TROY DEENEY

REDEMPTION

TROY DEENEY

with Oliver Holt

REDEMPTION

MY STORY

First published in Great Britain in 2021
by Cassell, an imprint of
Octopus Publishing Group Ltd
Carmelite House
50 Victoria Embankment
London EC4Y 0DZ
www.octopusbooks.co.uk

An Hachette UK Company
www.hachette.co.uk

Distributed in the US by
Hachette Book Group
1290 Avenue of the Americas
4th and 5th Floors
New York, NY 10104

Distributed in Canada by
Canadian Manda Group
664 Annette St.
Toronto, Ontario,
Canada M6S 2C8

ISBN 978-1-78840-276-7

A CIP catalogue record for this book is
available from the British Library.

Printed and bound in the
United Kingdom

10 9 8 7 6 5 4 3 2 1

This FSC® label means that materials
used for the product have been
responsibly sourced

Publisher: Trevor Davies
Editors: Ella Parsons & Sarah Kyle
Copy Editor: John English
Creative Director: Jonathan Christie
Typesetter: Jeremy Tilston
Production: Caroline Alberti,
Nic Jones & Lucy Carter

There are a lot of people to thank for their support during this crazy journey I've travelled so far in my life. In fact, too many to mention, so if you haven't been mentioned by name we both know why 😬.

But seriously, every person that's helped – from conversations to arguments – I appreciate you. Having said that, I have a few individuals without whom things could be very different and not in a good way. Firstly my mum, Emma, who's been a rock all my life and always been there for me. My father, Paul Anthony Burke, who you will read about, but who, regardless of his faults, loved and guided me in his way and gave me many of the traits that have made me what I am today.

My siblings Ellis, Sasha, Joel and Caiden, I'm proud of all of you and love you all more than you will know. My agent and friend, Simon Kennedy, who's been there through all my career highs and lows and always had my back. Disk, my closest friend, my right-hand man, you've done more for me than anybody would ever know. I love you to death.

Finally to the lady, my Queen, who literally changed my life for the better. Alisha, you brought the light to my brain and showed me what I'm truly capable of. This life will lead us down lots of crazy paths but I'm forever grateful that it's you walking side by side with me – I love you.

To my kids, you will never know the impact you've had on my life – you're the reason I get up and work so hard. I love you more than I can ever express.

CONTENTS

PROLOGUE: THE DEATH OF ME

Three people made me who I am today: Emma Deeney is my Mum and the strongest person I know. My Dad, Paul Anthony Burke, decided I should take my Mum's surname when I was a young child because he had the kind of reputation around Birmingham that made it better if I was not readily associated with him. Even though my Dad could be violent and abusive towards me and Mum, even though he was in and out of jail most of his life, he looked after me, he taught me how to be a man, he taught me how to play football and I knew that he loved me and that I loved him. And Colin Hemmings is my biological father.

They are what made me the way I am. The three of them. You don't really need to look much further than them to understand me.

Colin Hemmings was a hospital porter who wanted to be a DJ. He left me and my Mum when I was a baby and I have had very little to do with him since. Until recently, just hearing his name would make me feel angry. Rejection like that leaves a mark on a kid and on a man and, knowingly and unknowingly, I have been trying to deal with it for most of my life.

In the period of my life when I drank too much, a decade or so ago now, I thought I drank because I couldn't deal with death. When I was drinking the most, going straight from a nightclub in Birmingham to catch the 4.30am train out of New Street to

Watford Junction, sleeping in my car for a couple of hours at the Watford training ground before I went out to play football, I attributed it to the fact my Dad was dying from cancer.

But the root of my unhappiness, the core of the struggle I was having with myself, actually came a lot earlier in my life. I think of Colin Hemmings as a sperm donor. Nothing more. That was the only contribution he made to my life really. But his rejection left a mark on me that I can't get rid of no matter how hard I try to scrub it away.

And when my father passed away, who was the DJ at his wake? Colin Hemmings.

I know that 'surreal' is an overused word these days but I think that qualifies. It was incredibly weird. He came up to me a couple of times and I was thinking, 'This is really not the time.' He was trying to ask me if I was all right. 'Not really, no.' Some people said we look alike – my Mum always used to say it when she'd had a few drinks – and that really wound me up.

I'm good at forgetting. In fact, over the years, I've made myself an expert in forgetting. If you're in the same room as me and I'm not looking in your direction, you're not here. You're just a painting on the wall and I walk past you all the time. At the wake, a couple of people said to me: 'He looks like you, Troy.' And I said: 'Yeah, it's my Dad.' They said: 'But weren't we just burying your Dad?'

It's clear to me now that that first feeling of rejection is why I have always wanted to fit in. It's why I have always wanted to people-please, why I have wanted to be one of the lads, why I have wanted to be happy, why I have wanted everyone to like me, why I have seen it as my role to make people laugh, why I have never felt like I was good enough, why I have felt like an impostor, on and off the football pitch.

Someone chose to bring me into this world and then have nothing to do with me. And the reason he left couldn't have been anything to do with my Mum because everyone who has met Mum knows that she is a wonderful, strong woman. How can you not like my Mum? So I deduced from that that it must have been me. That's how I used to think about it: he must not have wanted me.

I know that's backwards thinking but that's how it was. A lot of things I have done are because of rejection. I have put this hard mask on, this tough guy who fights and brawls and gives no quarter and went to prison and told my family not to cry when the sentence was handed down and says the Arsenal players don't have 'cojones', all because I don't want to be rejected again.

Even the drinking comes back to rejection. I don't actually like to drink. I don't think anybody does. I don't think anybody picks up a pint of lager for the first time, drinks it and thinks, *That was better than water*. It's an acquired taste and just something that we do socially. No one likes it the first time. No one picks up a brandy and goes, *That didn't burn my chest*. So I never drank until I was 18.

But because everyone around me was drinking, I felt I had to drink or they wouldn't let me hang around with them. If you don't drink, you're going to be the weirdo. I used to drink because that's what everybody else was doing. I don't look at a brandy and think, *I can't wait to drink that.* But as soon as I have one, I'm all or nothing: I'm going to drink until I black out.

I also struggle with conflict resolution. People see Troy Deeney and think, *He's not scared of anything.* That's actually the opposite to the way I really am. I need a lot of reassurance in normal life. Football is where I have built this alter ego and I can be something else. The real me is very conscious of being classed as stupid. People say I'm a smart individual but I know I don't have the books smart. I'm more street smart.

When I do newspaper interviews, say, I'll maybe do an hour's worth of research as to who they are, who they have spoken to already, just so I don't go into a room not knowing. It's not for preparation. It's so I can go in a room and feel I belong. I know once I speak to someone for five minutes, I can gauge that person. But going into a boardroom or a financial meeting, I put people at an intellectual level above me because I haven't got that confidence.

If I like you, I will try my best not to argue with you. Even if I know I'm right, I'll say I'm wrong so I can't have an argument with you as I don't like what that does. I think that comes from my childhood sense of always wanting to fit in, always wanting to be someone's mate and always wanting to be accepted.

On a football pitch, I feel free. It's the only time I feel safe. I have ten other people with me, wanting the same thing. I view football as the perfect safety net. We are all striving for a common goal… to win. If you are part of a team and you are doing well and someone is passing to you and you are scoring goals and the fans are cheering you, you can't be that bad. I found I could be myself on the football pitch and people ended up liking me. I'm not the best footballer. I'm not the most athletic. I'm not the greatest with my right foot. But what I do, I'm good at, and people like it.

Rejection still runs deep. It causes me less pain than it used to, but I am still figuring it out. It still affects me and those around me. I don't talk. I try and talk and I try and have conversations, but sometimes I don't articulate myself very well, so people don't actually understand what I'm trying to say.

If I say to someone 'I'm not drinking any more because it creates problems for me,' I will say it in a way that people think I'm joking. I went to Watford's promotion party at the end of the 2020–21 season and made sure I didn't get there until the early evening when everyone was already hammered. I stayed for a little while and then slipped away. No one noticed.

There was alcohol and there was violence. I am wary of saying I had an unhappy childhood because there were a lot of great things in it and I wouldn't change the friends I made. I was lucky, too, because the man who I will always call 'Dad' took care of me when my biological father rejected me. But even though it sounds uncompromising my Dad was also a career criminal and an unpredictable man and, yes, there were occasions when he was violent towards my Mum and towards me.

I don't like violence but I am not afraid of it. When I was a younger man, I enjoyed a night out more if there was a fight at the end of it. It was the camaraderie of it, I suppose. It was the adrenaline. And it bonded people together. The problem is that because violence became normal to me, either witnessing it or being involved in it as a younger man, the consequences of it didn't actually hit home until later.

Violence took me to prison, too. At the end of February 2012, a couple of days after my Dad was diagnosed with terminal cancer, I got involved in another fight at the end of a night out on Broad Street in Birmingham. It ended with me kicking a student in the head when he was on the floor.

I could have dragged people away from the situation and said, 'Let's call it a day.' But my reaction to it was that we will have a fight, it will be what it is, and we will go to work the next day as if it was nothing. Naturally, it wasn't quite that simple. In June that year, I pleaded guilty to affray and was sentenced to ten months in jail. I felt ashamed of what I had done. My picture was plastered across the front of the local papers and I couldn't bear the shame I'd brought on my family.

This is a nasty side to me. I still struggle to control it. But I would be lying if I said that it wasn't a part of me. To give you an example…I might be on a night out and it's 8pm and we're having a bite to eat and someone asks for a picture and I'll say, 'Yeah, mate, no problem, no problem, no problem.' Then we go on somewhere else and somebody will ask again and I'll say, 'No problem, no problem, no problem.' And about 11pm, I've been taking pictures with everyone for three hours and then I'll say to my friends, 'Next time someone comes, we're going to stop doing the photos now, I want to enjoy myself before I go home.'

You're the next person who comes up and my pals will say, 'Listen, mate, he's had enough, he wants to enjoy himself.' And then they'll say, 'Ah, he thinks he's a big man, fuck him.' Then they'll look at me and they'll say, 'Who the fuck are you?' So I have to step in and either take a picture to de-escalate the situation or go, 'Listen, mate, this is why, please respect that.'

Because of my persona on the pitch, that person might want to engage or get a reaction. The problem is, with me, if you get that reaction out of me, you are not going to like it. I'm a big boy, I can handle myself, and I'm not afraid to square up with anyone. I do struggle with that side. I have road rage and the missus will ask, 'Why did you do that?' It's ingrained in me that someone is making fun of me and someone is making me feel vulnerable again.

I have never hit anyone just because. That's not me. I don't like bullies. I can't stand them for obvious reasons: my Dad bullied my Mum in many respects. I would never do that to somebody else. But if I feel personally attacked or violated, I have two ways to deal with it: I either remove myself from the situation or I engage. And if I engage, it is going to take the other person to back down before I will. Thus I'm battling with myself all the time.

I'm still trying to understand myself and deal with what happened to me when I was a kid. I've been having therapy ever since I came out of jail at the end of 2012. At first, it was because it was a condition of my release, but I found it helped me and I became intrigued by it. I stepped it up because what it initially did was peel back a layer of the onion. I am quite an inquisitive person so if I don't understand something, I want to know why. I hate the thought of not knowing something. I don't mean in the sense of relationship. I don't mean jealousy. If my missus has gone out and I don't know where she is, that's fine. Do whatever you've got to do. What I mean is I hate not having an understanding of self.

People get scared of truths. The more layers you peel away, the deeper it gets. And I haven't been good at dealing with my emotions, with feelings, so I am trying to get into that layer now which is very difficult and some tears come with the effort, but it's what I need to do to be a better parent and a better partner. Football is my life, I give everything to it, but I have 50 years after that to be a parent, hopefully grandparent, and partner. I want to be a nice guy, a good guy.

The human brain intrigues me. The way we act is all learned behaviour. We pick up everything from our parents, the way to be, the way to live. I grew up in Chelmsley Wood, which was the largest council estate in Europe. I'm not glamorizing it or saying I had the hardest life ever. I was loved. But you get older and look back and think, 'Ah, my Dad wasn't around that much.' I was always told he was on holiday, or working away, when in fact he was in jail. As a kid, you don't think about it so much, you just go off and play football. It's later that you think about the impact.

This is what happened to me. I had a good therapist and I'd talk for an hour and come out of it and think, *Why do I feel so tired?* I've unloaded a lot of things and not even understood what I've said.

Then the next session you'll come back and they break it down, what you said and why you said it. You start understanding your language and how you are talking.

I've come to realize that one of the keys to understanding and fixing myself is relationships. Trying to mend relationships that I broke through my behaviour when I was in my twenties. I was earning shedloads of money, drinking like a madman and I thought I could tell anyone what I wanted. I'm mending that and trying to get people to understand that that side of me is long gone.

I am actually quite a nice human now but if you only had interactions with me when I was out of my head on drink, thinking I was better than everybody else, you are only going to see that. If you did 99 good things, everyone remembers the one bad thing.

Emotions were all cut out for me when I was a kid. I never talked about emotions or feelings with anyone. When I analyse myself, I went through something that was traumatic at the age of nine involving my Dad attacking my Mum and me in the house and the police vans screeching up outside our flat and taking my Dad away. My Mum never cried in front of me and we never spoke about it in depth.

We have never talked things out, my Mum and me. It's not the way my family works. When I was working on this book, the two of us drove round some of our old haunts in Birmingham, some of the places we lived, my grandparents' house, the one that my Dad followed us to once, the place where he tried to strangle my Mum. And we did talk then. And I discovered things I hadn't known before.

There were happy memories, too: the little square of grass in the churchyard opposite my grandparents' house where I used to play football when I was a little kid. It felt as big as Wembley to me back then, but now I look at it and it isn't much bigger than a postage stamp. But when I look further down that street, I see nightmarish things, too.

My Dad spent his life in and out of jail and Mum would tell me and my brother and sister that he had gone on holiday but after he attacked us, he was away for longer. When he came out of jail, we didn't know he was being released. We went to get petrol at a local filling station and a bus pulled up. When it pulled away, we looked over and he was just standing there. And my Mum gave him a lift.

Life just carried on. I am sure she must have shed plenty of tears but we never saw them. To me she is the toughest woman alive because of how she would not let anyone see her cry. After everything he did and the ways she suffered and how hard she worked. So I thought, *If she can't cry, my job is to make her happy.*

So I used to sing because I knew when I sang it would make her happy. I used to sing R&B songs until my balls dropped and then my vocals went out of the window. Until then, my Mum used to enjoy me singing so we would have music around. There was a garage record that I bought for her with money I won at school.

At school, I never really had fights. I was always the funny guy. Once I realized I could make people laugh, it transformed my school life. The people I hung around with were the best at sport and the hardest ones in the year, that was my social group. I could play football and I could fight, but the way I fitted into that group was by being the funny one.

I reckon in most groups of boys at school, there's the footballer, the hard man, the ladies' man, the lazy one and the funny man. I was the funny man. I used to see people wanting to hang around with us. And I saw that and it made me think I needed to stay in with that group. I got kicked out of lessons because I needed to be the funny guy, when ultimately I was just being a twat.

I think I've grown up now. I think I'm a better person than I was. What am I dealing with now? Where do you want me to start? Emotions, mainly. Understanding that if someone is upset and is crying, not necessarily from something I've done, but probably from something I've done, then some sympathy from me might be useful.

When I was a kid, if I fell over and scraped my leg and started crying, my Dad would say to me, 'Stop crying or I'll give you a reason to cry.' That was more normal back then. At least, I think it was more normal. That was the school I was brought up in. Now the times are completely different. My kids don't need to be tough. I don't want my kids to be tough. I want my kids to be connected emotionally.

I need therapy because how am I supposed to tell them to be something and I don't understand it? That's what I'm dealing with. Things like that. Connecting with my partner. Understanding that she thinks a different way to me. That doesn't mean she's wrong. It doesn't mean I'm right. Sometimes, there is a grey area.

Sometimes, you have to concede you're not right.

Within football, your teammates are your first opponent. I am battling them every day. Say the formation is 4-5-1, which means there are three or four strikers trying to get in the team. So every day you are trying to beat that person who is actually on your team. You can transfer that into your relationship, and that's the danger.

Every relationship needs a dominant person in different fields. Let's say I bring in more money than my missus. She can't help that. But I can't use the computer as well as she can. There are a lot of things I can't do as well as her. In certain aspects, I need to be dominant, in other aspects she needs to be dominant. In football, you are conditioned to be totally dominant. So I'm working on understanding the emotions that are attached to that and understanding that football isn't real life.

I've done a lot in football. I've played in each of the four divisions. I've seen what life's like at the bottom and the top. When I started out at Walsall, on loan to Halesowen Town, I was paid a few quid a week, which I collected in a brown paper envelope in the clubhouse. For a lot of the time I've been at Watford, I've earned more money than I could ever have imagined.

I've played at Merthyr Tydfil and I've played in an FA Cup final. I've gone to work with my boots in a plastic bag from Asda and I've shaken hands with Prince William on the turf at Wembley. I've helped to co-ordinate the players' fight against racism, I've scored important goals and I've done stupid things, but I'm still trying. I am not going to say I've got it right. I've effed up more than most people and I will again, but I am certainly trying. I'll have that on my gravestone: 'I went out trying.'

I mentioned in an interview with *The Times* recently that the old me would have called me an idiot for trying to deal with all of this psychology, for trying to understand the way I act like I do, for trying to improve the way I am. The old me would have called it pointless and pretentious. The old me would have laughed about it. Or, worse than that, said, 'Who the fuck are you trying to be?' But my psychologist said something that hit home really well. 'To become a new person, the old you has to die.'

CHAPTER 1

ALL KIPPERS AND CURTAINS

It was a Monday morning. It was early and I was still in bed. I was seven or eight years old. Mum, Dad and I and my younger brother, Ellis, lived in a first-floor flat in an 11-storey tower block called Keble House in Chelmsley Wood, eight miles east of Birmingham city centre. I learned to ride my bike on the grassy bank out the front that backed onto Chapelhouse Road.

I liked it there. I lived in Chelmsley Wood until I was 23. There was a solid sense of community. Some people would call it rough. Or deprived. But for me, it was a good upbringing. Everybody had very little and we all shared what we had. We had Woolworths and Iceland and Kwik Save, no Debenhams. We got a Greggs just before I moved out and I thought we were going up in the world.

My Mum often worked three jobs at a time, anything that would keep our heads above water. She worked at Aldi for a while, she cleaned the local Ladbrokes, pulled pints in pubs. We weren't poor in the sense we couldn't get shoes but we didn't have much. We had a TV with a pound slot on the side. A pound would give you three hours of TV. Gas and electric were on a meter, too.

There was a lot of excitement when we got a Nintendo 64 for Christmas when I was 13 or 14. Then our house got broken into on Boxing Day and we lost that. My Dad caught the person who did it. Actually, there were two people. What ensued from that, I don't know. I was never told that story. Snitches get stitches... something like that. I was too young, so wouldn't have known.

Anyway, it was about 6am on that Monday morning, I think. Our school was St Anne's Roman Catholic primary school. It was just around the corner so we always left it until the last minute to get out of the flat. Usually, we'd be up around ten past eight, have a quick wash, brush our teeth and head out so we'd get to school for half past. That morning was different. We got an early alarm call.

I woke out of my sleep. I heard some sort of commotion outside on the landing our front door. I had no idea what it was. It sounded like some sort of rumbling. Then I could hear voices. Ellis and I had bunk beds and our bedroom was off a long corridor that ran from the front door into the flat so the noise travelled fast.

I didn't get up. I was still in a kind of daze, but I realized that my Dad must be standing close to our front door. It sounded like he was talking to somebody through it. Then I heard him laughing and taunting whoever it was on the other side. It was the police, but I didn't know that at the time and my Dad didn't give away any clues. He certainly didn't sound scared. I never saw him scared of anyone.

The rumbling that I heard grew sharper and became a kind of hammering. My Mum said they were trying to bang down our door. My Dad was still laughing, teasing them for not being able to get in straight away. Then the commotion got louder and our front door sort of collapsed and fell back in on itself. Bodies piled through it like they were extras in a zombie movie.

My Dad had been laughing at them and as they came through the door, he must have taken a couple of steps back because he ended up in line with the door to our bedroom. He would never have gone peacefully and simply. I think he enjoyed the tussle and making it difficult for them. It's not like it would have been a terrible day for him. This was almost routine.

In the melee in the hall, the door to our bedroom got smashed off its hinges, too. I was in the top bunk and I looked down. I was a kid. I was scared. I shouted out to him but he told me everything was fine and that this was just role play. 'No, don't worry, son,' he said, 'go back to sleep. It's fine, Dad's just playing with his mates.'

I stared down at the scene that was unfolding. My Dad was lying there, face down in the hall, with policemen swarming all round him. One had his right arm, one his left arm, one his right foot and one his left. And they picked him up like that, spread-eagled, and carried him down our narrow corridor and out on to the first floor landing. I went back to sleep.

The thing was, I was naïve enough to believe he was actually mucking around with his mates. He always made us feel safe. I didn't know it then, but that was the first time I'd witnessed him getting arrested. I knew that he got in trouble. I knew that he went away sometimes. Mum, of course, never let on he was in jail.

That morning when the police smashed down our door, it was to arrest him for something that was really fairly inconsequential. My Mum thinks it was that he hadn't paid a fine of some sort, that he had let it slide and slide and ignored warning after warning, and in the end, the fine had grown into a criminal charge and there was a warrant out for his arrest, so the police had come round. It was nothing glamorous. It wasn't like he'd robbed a bank.

Everything was casual for him. When I was a young player trying to make my way at Walsall, Dad came to watch me play in an away game at Northampton Town. When I came out of the ground after the match, he was waiting for me in a blue Mercedes. I knew he didn't have a blue Mercedes. He didn't have a car. He didn't even have a licence. He had never passed his test. He had never taken his test.

I assumed the Mercedes had been 'borrowed' but I got in and we set off down the M1. He had the music turned up loud and everything was cool and we were chatting about the game. Then we stopped somewhere to get petrol. The music went off when he switched off the ignition and I heard this banging coming from somewhere behind me.

I looked around into the back seat and I couldn't see anything. I thought another car had bumped into us.

'Can you hear that noise, Dad?' I said.

He said: 'Yeah, don't worry about that.'

'What do you mean?'

'Look,' he said, 'there's someone in there but I'm going to drop him off in a bit.'

He mentioned the name of a bloke who was known as a small-time drug-dealer on the estate.

'What?'

'He owes my pal some money so I've taken him on a little journey for the day,' Dad said. 'I've fed him and that and he's fine. We'll drop him off later and I bet he pays.'

'What?'

There was me trying to make a career at Walsall and we are driving round with a bloke in the boot of the car. To him, that was normal. He led two different lives. Every time he got nicked or got into a scrap, it added to this mystique and this legend of who he was. His way of thinking about it was *What's the worst they're going to do, lock me up again?* If he did six or twelve months somewhere in jail, that was easy.

That was the kind of offender he was, really. It was a way of life. It wasn't unusual for him not to be there. That wasn't always because he was locked up. It was often that we just didn't know where he was. It was usually for four or six weeks when he was locked up and when he came back, he would make it seem as if you'd seen him yesterday. He acted like nothing had happened. It wasn't much fun for my Mum.

We knew he had a temper, but never towards us. Not then. Not yet. It was always outside the house. I wasn't scared of him. Not then. Not yet. The other kids weren't, either. My Dad was great with kids, the kind of Dad who was really good at making sure everyone plays football. If you went to a family party and there was one adult that always played with the kids and went on the bouncy castle, my Dad was that guy in the community. He would come out and play football with us for hours. He'd get bottles of water for us all. He'd make sure every kid played.

I remember random things. He used to take us to pubs. They have all been knocked down and turned into McDonald's now. There was a pub across the bridge from us that was called the Roundhouse. There was a big grass field outside it. We'd go and play football outside and I knew Dad would be inside and he might see us and we might get 50p to go to the shop.

When we were around there, we saw the respect my Dad had. People would come out and go, 'You're Burkey's son, aren't you?', and we wouldn't say anything and they'd say, 'Here's a pound'. My Dad would come out and he'd say, 'Don't give them anything' and he'd say to me, 'If someone offers you money, say no unless it's me or your Mum.'

Later in my life, when I played my first game for Walsall, we went back to a pub Dad grew up in and he walked in proud as punch because of what I'd done. 'Right,' he said, 'who's buying me and my son a drink?' I said ,'Dad, I'll get us a drink, I'm earning £50 a week now.' I thought I was loaded. He said, 'No, we never pay for drinks here.'

My Dad was so much about respect and people fearing him and his name. There was a kind of formality about him in that way. When he was first introduced to someone, he thought it was right that he should be addressed by his full name, Paul Anthony Burke.

He was meticulous about extending the same courtesy to others. That rubbed off on me. I won't call someone by their Christian name until I've met them several times.

He taught me that your last name is your first name. Your family name is your most important name. So how people see your family name is how people see you before they even meet you. He wanted people to know who he was. My Dad did not have fancy cars or gold chains, but he made sure his name created respect.

He wasn't the kind of criminal who made millions. I couldn't even really put a label on what he did that got him into so much trouble. He got into a lot of fights, particularly after he had had a drink. I've seen him referred to as a drug-dealer in some of the profiles that have been written about me and maybe he did do a bit of that, but if he did, it was only small-time stuff. He sold knock-off stuff here and there, I think he probably acted as a kind of enforcer for people now and again. He didn't care about the law, really. He ignored it and then every so often, it caught up with him.

A lot of my Dad's friends are millionaires off whatever they've done. He had bugger all. He never wanted the money. He enjoyed a tear-up. He enjoyed creating fear. He enjoyed walking in somewhere and someone going, 'Fuck, there's Burkey.' He was never in a gang. He had a group of mates he grew up with, another group of lads he went to the football with, and everyone knew him, but if anyone needed something doing, they went to him.

He was so engaging. That was why he was so good at selling things on the street, because you would want to talk to him. He was like the guy you see selling Sky in a shopping centre. He did cash-in-hand jobs. But there was something about him that could make you uneasy, too. You know when you look at certain people and they have a little look in their eye and you think, *Oh, you're not wired properly.* There would be something little and he would switch and you couldn't stop it.

Emotionally, I'm very detached. My Dad was a lovely man in many ways but my Mum used to say to me that every time he went out, she worried about whether he'd ever come back. Whether he'd be locked up. Whether he'd end up dead. That worry must have rubbed off on me, too. I still have trouble emotionally investing. At some level, it's because my Dad was in and out of our lives.

He would get into fights daily when he was in his heyday. With anyone. Someone who owed him money. Someone who may have owed a friend money. You knew if he was coming for you. He was so blasé about it, he would call you and say he was coming. He would say he would be at the house in 15 minutes to collect the money. And if you didn't have the money, he'd collect you.

He did a bit of everything. We got bikes when I was 12. I had been riding mine around the estate for about a week and someone knocked on the door, a man and his child. My Dad had sold drugs to someone and in order to pay him, this geezer had stolen a kid's bike, and given it to my Dad instead of cash. The kid had seen me riding his bike round the estate and now they were at our door. My Dad gave the bike back. He wasn't your nasty, vindictive kind of criminal.

All he needed was a few quid in his pocket to sort my Mum out, sort us kids out and then be off. He was uncomfortable with money so if somebody gave him five grand, he would have to give it away. He didn't like clothes or designer brands. He could dress smartly, go to the pub and be in the mix, but didn't like owning houses or cars.

The night he met my Mum for the first time, he had just got out of jail after doing time for grievous bodily harm. He was taking the rap for someone else, he said. He wasn't guilty, he said. He never was. Some of his friends had big houses and he used to say, 'Yeah, they might have that, but it's all kippers and curtains.'

I looked that phrase up once. I think it meant they might have a big house with a lovely façade and fancy curtains in a nice area, but all they could afford to eat were kippers. It was all a front that concealed the reality. And then there was us. We might be living in a council flat, but we're having salmon for dinner. I don't remember us having salmon for dinner, but I understand what he was getting at.

Before Mum left him, the only time I saw him get violent was when he played Sunday league football. He'd have one of those Nurishment chocolate drinks for his breakfast, washed down with a brandy, and if he scored a goal, he liked to do one of his repertoire of celebrations. His favourite was the Lee Sharpe one where he danced with the corner flag.

This particular Sunday, he asked me and my brother which celebration he should do that day. He had already scored two and he had done the Lee Sharpe celebration and then the Cantona one with his collar up. Then one of the opposition team players said something – I think it was racist because there were only a couple of things that would make him go instantly – and he whacked this geezer. I have never seen anyone hit the floor harder.

And then he whacked anyone that came near him and it took four or five of his mates to restrain him. I think he got banned from football and arrested because of that. The thing that struck me was that he had hit all these people and then in the next instant, as he was walking off the pitch, he looked over at me and said: 'Troy, grab your coat, we'll go and get a beer inside, okay, mate?'

That one really did my head in. How do you go from absolute anger and rage to borderline serial killer, cool and calculating, chilled as if nothing has happened? Bang, in an instant. He didn't legally drive so we had one of his pals driving. I was allowed a Nurishment in a tin can as a treat. It came with the message that I had better not tell Mum what had happened. Certain things didn't get said, not even to my Mum. It was a family thing. We just didn't speak about it.

Dad preferred playing football to watching. He was a Leeds fan, for some reason I never really understood, although I suppose that his youth would have coincided with the period when Leeds were in their pomp under Don Revie. I don't remember ever going to watch Leeds, though, but he did take me to watch Birmingham City every so often.

His main interest in going to St Andrew's was the tribal nature of it. He was a member of the Zulus, the name given to the hardcore part of the Blues' supporters. I read that they got their name because of their multicultural following. Most of the hooligan 'firms' of the seventies and eighties had a far-right, skinhead element. It was underpinned by white supremacy. But it wasn't like that at Birmingham and so opposing fans thought they could insult them by calling them Zulus.

The Zulus began in the eighties. They might have ended up as a hooligan group but they started out as my Dad and his mates. I've read books about them and when I look at the pictures, there's my Dad with a few of my 'Uncles'. To begin with, it was intended as a defence mechanism against skinheads and the National Front. Birmingham City had a skinhead culture. The Black Birmingham City fans used to get attacked by their own fans so the Zulus was formed to stick up for themselves and have safety in numbers.

Once the hooliganism started, they latched on to that, too. My Dad would go to an away game in Cardiff, say, and he and his mates would go in a van, head to the local shopping centre, rob the shops, get as much stuff as they could, put it in the van, go and watch the game, have a tear-up, come home, sell all the stuff that was in the van, women's clothes that they had managed to grab and run. To him, that was a good weekend.

He'd watched the football, had a weekend with the lads and put a few quid in his pocket. They'd grab videos, clothes, quick-fix stuff. There might be one security guard on the door. The policing was much more lax in those days. There is so much CCTV now, and forensics. It would be impossible to get away with stuff like that today. They wouldn't even have got out of the car park at the shopping centre. Number plate recognition would have done for them, apart from anything else.

I never went on those away trips but Dad took me to home games in the mid-nineties sometimes when there was a kid-for-a-quid promotion. I never really saw the violence. My Dad wouldn't take us when he was planning to have a scrap. We'd go to the safer, lesser games. Not Cardiff, Villa, Millwall, Leeds, Wolves, West Brom or West Ham. Those were the games when it was likely to kick off. I wasn't allowed anywhere near those games.

The Zulus were a tight-knit crew but when they had disagreements, they were not for the faint-hearted. My Dad had a real love–hate relationship with one particular guy he had known since they were big mates at school. This mate of his was the businessman and my Dad was the hoodlum and they worked well together for many years. I'm not going to mention his name, by the way. I just think it would be wiser not to.

Then they fell out. I was told my Dad was selling Ecstasy at some festival or concert that his mate had organized and he was doing it without his permission. Not only that, but the Ecstasy wasn't actually Ecstasy. It was just paracetamol. My Dad had scratched the P off the tablets and so he was making a huge profit on any he sold. So they fell out over money, basically.

People had to take sides and most of the Zulus stayed with my Dad's mate because he had the money and so he had the power. But they were scared of my Dad. It must have been a tough choice. They invited him to a pub near Stechford, which is close to where the TV series *Peaky Blinders* is set, but when he got there, he discovered it was a trap.

The Pelham Arms was an old establishment hostelry. You went in through double doors and then there was a short passageway leading to another set of double doors that swung open into the main body of the pub. When he walked through the first set of double doors, they trapped my Dad in this little walkway where the doors closed. They filled him in.

I spoke to some of the people who were there when I was writing my Dad's eulogy and they said he was the strongest bastard they'd ever met in their lives. And he was stubborn, too. There were eight or nine of them against him and they told him they were just going to teach him a lesson but he looked everyone in the eye and said, 'You better hope you kill me because I'm going to get you back.'

They beat him for 40 minutes, but he kept getting up. They asked him to stay down but he wouldn't. He kept getting up until they gave up and figured he had been taught enough of a lesson. He phoned from a phone box and told my Mum to run him a bath and walked home, battered and bruised. He got up the next day and went to the pub with a potato peeler in his back pocket. He waited for every single one of them to come back in. Our families avoided each other for many, many years after that.

They settled it in the end. When my Dad was dying, word got around that he only had a very short time to live and this old mate of his turned up at the house. I thought, *What the fuck is he doing here?* But my Uncle was in the Zulus and he took me aside and explained this guy just wanted to pay his respects. There was a moment where everyone went out of the room and left the two men alone. My Dad gasped some words out and their feud was over.

CHAPTER 2

NO GOING BACK

When my Mum was 17, she worked as a carer at East Birmingham Hospital in Bordesley Green. She liked working on the geriatric ward because a lot of the old folks loved to chat. She filled their water jugs and brought them sandwiches and kept them company. There was a social club at the hospital and one Friday night, a friend of hers persuaded her to go to the disco there. That's when she met Colin Hemmings, my biological father.

He was a hospital porter and a part-time DJ. He had mates called Gary and Tony so for music purposes, they called themselves CGT. Mum went to the disco a few times and one New Year's Eve, Colin Hemmings asked her if she wanted to go to a party afterwards. He already had a baby with someone else but Mum didn't know that until much later.

After they had been going out for some time, Mum found out she was expecting me and while she was pregnant, Colin Hemmings was offered a job as a DJ in Ibiza. He thought he was going to make it big but he ended up playing to a few stragglers in some poxy bar. Mum took me over there to see him for my first birthday, but she soon found out he had been seeing other women and so she split up with him. My Mum's very loyal but when she's done, she's done. There's no going back.

Some months later, Mum met Paul Anthony Burke at a house party. His way of chatting her up was taking her hand, putting a Rizla in her palm and making a spliff. Really romantic. He asked Mum if she smoked and she said she didn't smoke weed. 'Good girl, are we?' my Dad said. He had only been out of jail for a few weeks after serving time for GBH.

It wasn't easy being in a mixed-race relationship in those days, but Mum's family was a great example of the mixing of cultures. Her Nan had married an Irishman, which had been frowned upon by some of her relatives at the time, so she couldn't stand anyone being a racist or a bigot. When her own daughter, my Mum's Aunt, started going out with a Black guy, she made sure she welcomed him.

This guy would come and pick my Great Auntie Marie up to take her out for the evening, but because he was aware that some people in the family thought it was wrong for her to be going out with him, he would park his car at the bottom of the hill a few hundred yards away and wait for her there. My Nan found out about this and one night, she took my Mum, who was a young girl then, by the hand and walked down the hill to see this guy.

She introduced herself to him and told him that if he had come to take her daughter out for a drink, then he was going to come inside and say hello to everybody. She was the kindest person. She had the mentality that nobody was going to be left out and nobody was going to be discriminated against. My Mum had the same attitude.

Mum said that we didn't see Colin Hemmings for dust after they split up. Sometimes, he would make an arrangement to come and pick me up around the time when I was two or three, Mum said, and I'd be waiting at the window with my little rucksack on my back and he wouldn't turn up. Or he'd be four hours late and I'd be too upset by then to go out anyway.

My Mum and Dad were living together by then and it upset my Dad to see the effect it had on me when Colin Hemmings didn't turn up. Things came to a head when my Mum asked Colin Hemmings for some financial support in raising me and he offered my Mum £5 to buy a pair of trainers for me. My Dad went round and had a word with him. I imagine it wasn't a particularly friendly conversation.

I know he told him that I got upset when he didn't turn up and because I got upset, then my Mum got upset too. And he told him that the offer of £5 was an insult. He told him that if he wasn't prepared to take the responsibility of being my Dad then he'd take the responsibility for him. He told him that if he wanted to visit, that was fine, but that if he didn't want to, he shouldn't bother. 'So he didn't bother,' my Mum said. 'He literally didn't bother.'

And so from then on, my real Dad, Paul Anthony Burke, was always around for me. He wanted my brother, Ellis, and my sister, Sasha, to have the same name as my Mum because his last name got him into trouble around Birmingham. If you were known as a

Burke, you were known as somebody. And not in a good way. So my name was changed from Troy Hemmings to Troy Deeney by deed poll when I was about 18 months old.

I have never really had much contact with Colin Hemmings. There was a time, when I was around 14 or 15, when I wanted to see him. I had had some ups and downs with my Dad and, as a teenager, you start getting curious and wondering what's what, so my Mum sorted it out for me to see Colin Hemmings and he picked me up.

It was weird. He drove me round to his place. He had another son sitting in the front seat while I was in the back and they were laughing and joking with each other and it was clear they had a good relationship and I was some kind of afterthought. We got to his house and he introduced me to a few people who were there and then left.

He left me in a house with a load of family members who were strangers to me. A couple of hours later, I called my Mum and asked her to come and get me. That was the end of my curiosity really. I never asked to see him again.

As I mentioned, I did see him at my Dad's funeral. The two of them had been friends at one point. They were both from Small Heath and so they had a lot of friends in common and knew a lot of the same people. That was how he ended up being the DJ at my Dad's wake.

That was a weird night. I was struggling with my Dad's death and all the issues about my inability to show any emotion and then suddenly there's Colin Hemmings playing the tunes and doing his spiel and wandering over and asking if I'm okay. I didn't want to talk to him. It wasn't the time or the place. To be honest, I don't think it will ever be the time or the place.

The last time I saw him, it was six or seven months before my first child was born and it was thought it might be a good idea if he came round to my flat. Colin Hemmings treated it like a public-relations stunt.

His mum's American and all he seemed to want to do was take some photos of us all together so that he could send them to her. I suppose he wanted to give her the impression that we were one big happy family and this was him with his son who loved him and was looking forward to him becoming the grandfather to his child. It was a sham.

When we asked if we were going to meet up again, there were loads of excuses and the second he left, I said to my partner at the time, 'Don't ever ask for that to happen again.' I have only had two or three encounters with him in my 33 years and none of them has lasted longer than a couple of hours, so, like I said, he is just a sperm donor to me.

He left my Mum when she was 19 years old to fend for herself. That's not a man to me. I have contempt for him. He is not for me. He took the piss out of my Mum. I am sure he is still saying to people that I am his son and trying to get some form of credit for it and the best he could offer was a fiver for some shoes.

I hate the fact that he might use me as some sort of reference because the only contribution he made to my life after my birth has been negative. By that I mainly mean the feeling of rejection I've already referred to. I am a people-pleaser because of that fear of not being good enough. There might be something I don't want to do but I'll do it if it makes that person like me rather than turning them down.

It affects my relationships as well. I am not very good emotionally. I have never had a Dad putting an arm round me and showing me the ropes. My Dad was very much old school in so far as you couldn't cry. If things get difficult, I just close up. Maybe I get that from Colin Hemmings. When things got difficult, he ran off. There are traits and learned behaviours.

He's around. I don't speak to him or reach out for him. He ditched me so I wasn't good enough for him then so I'm certainly not good enough now. I can't change someone's actions. Has it caused me pain over the years? A hundred per cent. Of course it has. I have spoken to psychologists about how that has impacted my life in regard to my children and why I used to drink so much.

Until about two years ago, if you mentioned his name, I would start getting really angry and bubbling up, but now I have spoken to my Mum more about it. If she doesn't get wound up by it, then I don't really have a right to either.

My Mum feels sorry for him, I think. He has got other kids. He has a sad existence. A lot of the stuff he was doing 25 years ago, he is still doing now. I have technically got an older brother and a younger sister but I don't have anything to do with any of them. I have got my brothers and sisters on this side of the fence and that's it.

My Dad was a rogue, a chancer, whatever you want to call him. He spent time in jail. He did some bad things. And he did some bad things to me, too. But that doesn't change the basic equation for me where he and I are concerned. In that respect, the story is simple: he took me on when my biological father didn't want me. He told Colin Hemmings: 'I'm the man now, you're not doing your job.'

He looked after me, taught me how to play football, taught me how to defend myself, taught me what was right and wrong, taught me how to ride a bike, how to swim. My Granddad was a brown belt in karate and he took me to martial arts and my Dad would smack me round the head and got me into shadow boxing and holding my fist properly.

He told me that I must never be a bully, which was ironic given the way he tried to bully my Mum on occasions. But anyway, it was a good thing to preach and I have tried to abide by it. I hate bullies. And he told me: 'Don't ever start something, but if someone brings it your way, make sure you finish it.'

For a guy who was fast and loose with the law, he was a stickler for rules round the house. We had that television I mentioned where you used to have to put a pound in the side to watch anything. If he was watching the telly, he would leave a pound on the top for the next person to use it. It was like a ritual for him and he expected everyone else to observe it, too.

One Saturday, it all went wrong. When my brother and I were kids we'd play football with our mates all day on Saturday and and on this occasion the other kids were asking if we could go out. My

Dad blocked the door and said: 'Where's the pound off the telly?'

I said: 'I ain't took it.' He said: 'Did you rob it?' He said: 'No one's going anywhere until you find that pound.' All the kids outside were playing football and we were looking and looking for hours. We were crying in the end because we had looked everywhere. Eventually, he went: 'Oh fuck, my fault, sorry. I put it in last night and fell asleep.' So he gave us both two pounds each as penance. It was the principle of you don't steal from family. It was only a pound, but it meant a lot to him even though he had four in his pocket.

Then there was food. I was the fussiest eater you have seen in your life. I lived on beans on toast and I had to have ketchup with everything. I didn't like cheese either. In fact, I didn't really like much at all apart from beans on toast. Until I went to jail, there were only three meals I would eat. When I went to jail, I had no choice but to eat different things, otherwise I would have starved.

One time, Dad made a pizza for me. I said I didn't like pizza. He said: 'You'll sit there until you eat it because it cost £2.50.' I thought I'd wait it out and pick at it. He sat there for four hours until I had eaten every piece of the pizza. It was about 10pm and I was falling asleep but he was firm…'No, fucking eat the pizza.'

People might think it was harsh. People will almost certainly think it was hypocritical given some of the stuff he got up to. But it was to teach the value of how much that pizza cost. My Mum had bought it and he said: 'Do you know how long your Mum had to work to pay for that?' She was probably only on about £4 an hour then.

Dad was also the inspiration for my football career. When I was six or seven and starting to show a little bit of promise, we walked around the whole of the area with a football, with my Dad saying to people: 'Can he play for your team, give him ten minutes and he will show you.'

I was never fast as a kid. I've never been fast as an adult. But he was always comparing me to Teddy Sheringham and telling anyone who would listen that I could read the game well. My first team was known as the 3Cs, which stood for Catholic Community Centre and they were the best team in our area. We went four years without losing.

My first game was for the Under-9s when I was six, just so Dad could get me a game. I played centre-half on a big pitch. My Dad said I hadn't really run enough so we did extra runs after the game. That was how my Dad approached things. He was the reason that me, my brother and sister were good at sports. My Mum wanted us to do stuff for the enjoyment of it. My Dad wanted us to be good at it.

If we're going to do it, we're going to be good at it. That was his attitude. He saw sport as a way out for us so he pushed us ridiculously hard. My sister was six or seven and going to gymnastics regularly and doing the splits and back bends and had a six pack and everything. It got to the point where even Ellis and I were telling him to give her a break.

Sometimes, we'd be in the house and he'd get a tennis ball and say: 'Right 20 keepy-uppies' and you couldn't do anything else until you'd done it. Even if you wanted to watch something on telly. If he felt you needed to do more, you were going to do more. I think we were all grateful for it in the end because we all learned a level of discipline that got us to a certain level of success within our lives.

He was good as a player, my Dad, and he was rapid as well. He used to say that if he could get away from the police, he could certainly get away from a defender. He made us believe that we could succeed at sport even if the odds were against it. When things don't seem achievable or attainable, your dreams die with it. I see it a lot now. I see people who are good but they look at their prospects of making it as a professional and they say, 'Those things don't happen to us.' They kill it in their own head before somebody else can kill it.

Mum and Dad stayed together for eight years until eventually Mum had had enough. I don't think it was the life of crime itself that wore her down, more the continued absences that were a part of that and the endless disruption that brought to her own life and to our life as a family. When she tried to end the relationship, though, he didn't take it well.

My Mum had given birth to Sasha by then and she'd passed her driving test. She had a little Maestro, which her Dad had bought for her and which was her pride and joy. She had a regular job at Aldi on the checkouts and she was carving out a good existence for herself and for us. But my Dad didn't really buy into that kind of existence.

I spoke to Mum about it recently.

'Paul used to drive,' she said, 'but he had never taken a test. My car was legal and insured and he kept taking it. I told him I needed it for work. I'd get up in the morning and he would have already gone. If I was on an early shift at Aldi, I'd have to be there for 7am so I'd have to get up, realize he'd taken the car, get a taxi to my Mum's and do a shift from 7am until 7pm.

'Then my Mum would pick the children up from school and so I'd go back to my Mum's and everyone would be there but then I'd have to get the bus home. And I'd get home and Paul would be asleep on the settee and my car would be sat outside and I was like, "You're taking the piss." My Dad bought me that car when I passed my test and I loved that Maestro. I polished it to death.

'I could cope with it most of the time. Some of the stuff made me laugh. I was on the till at Aldi one day and I saw a guy in the store that I recognized as a friend of Paul's. He came through to the till and he was looking me in the eyes and he had a 42-inch TV underneath his trolley and he was basically trying to say to me "You haven't seen it", without actually saying it.

'He kept saying, "I know Paul, we're really good friends." And I said, "I don't care, It's my job." I just pressed the bell for security and they came and arrested him. Your Dad wasn't happy. He wasn't happy with his friend. He kept saying to him: "Why would you put her in that position?"

'Then things snowballed. He went off to the Glastonbury festival one year and took my car. He asked if he could borrow it and I said no, but he took it anyway and then I couldn't get hold of him and he came back on the Monday afternoon. He came back covered in mud and he wanted to know what my problem was. He had taken all my rent money and I said I couldn't cope with it any more.

'It escalated from there. I told him he needed to go. I told him I didn't need him for anything any more. I didn't need the hassle. I didn't need him messing me about. I didn't need him spending the kids' money. "You just need to go." He turned that around and said: "You need to go." I said, "Okay, I will." So I started to pack the kids' stuff and he wasn't having that.

'Looking back, I know he did care about me and I do think he actually loved me, but I just think he didn't know how to show it. He didn't know how to be a partner to somebody. He needed to be the strong Black man.

'We lived on the first floor and you went down two flights of steps and there was a shop. Ellis came up with a roll of black bags and he started packing my stuff. I started crying because he wouldn't let me get the kids' stuff together. He started saying, "You're leaving us" and he was twisting it around. He threatened me. He said he was taking the kids over to where there was a game of football and he said he wanted me gone before they all got back.

'He hit me while we were having a conversation together. I called the kids in because I didn't think he would hit me in front of them. But he did. When he hit me, it was always a punch but never in the face where you'd see it. A dig in the ribs or in the arm. He said he could have hit me a lot harder if he had wanted to.

'I knew I just had to get out of the flat. I was worried about what he might do, not just to me but to the kids, too. He was unpredictable.

And he couldn't bear not getting his own way. He was used to intimidating people. I hated leaving the kids there but I knew he would never harm them and I thought I'd come back and get them when everything calmed down.

'He put the kids on the balcony and showed them me driving away. It was often psychological with him. He preferred that game. I went to my Mum's with some of my clothes. I was absolutely distraught. I got to my Mum's and she had a friend there from the church and I was sobbing. My Mum told me he wouldn't keep the children. It was just that it was the only way he could hurt me.

'He got the children to ring me. He said: "Ring your Mum and say goodbye to your Mum because you're never going to see her again." And so you were crying and saying: "Why have you left?" and I was saying: "I haven't left but your Dad's not being very nice." He'd go through the same routine with Ellis.

'I tried to speak to him again. I was still distraught but he sounded cold on the other end of the line. "If you come anywhere near us," he said, "I'll kill you."'

CHAPTER 3

THE END OF INNOCENCE

Not long after Mum left, Sasha developed conjunctivitis. She was still a baby and she cried and cried and cried. Dad took her to the doctor, but she was still in a lot of discomfort. She wasn't sleeping too much and after another couple of weeks, Dad cracked and took us all round to my Nan's where Mum had been living. He said she could have us back.

But he was still desperately unhappy about the situation. He wanted us all to live together again but Mum would not change her mind. When they had split up, he had told her that if he took me and my brother and sister or went anywhere near us, he'd batter her in front of us. That hadn't happened, but there was still a sense of foreboding about the situation. Dad hadn't accepted things had changed.

I loved living at my Nan's house. It felt like freedom. Not freedom from my Dad because I didn't want to be free from him. I loved him. But the freedom to be a kid, the freedom not to have to play a role, the freedom to play with toys that we never had at home, the freedom to play in a garden and live in a house. It was a house in a terraced street, Lyttleton Road, in Stechford, but it felt like a palace to me.

It felt like a sanctuary. And then one day that sanctuary was invaded. I felt like my childhood ended that day really and that things in our family would never be the same again. They couldn't be, really, not when your day turned into a something like a scene from a horror movie.

Mum came to pick me up from school that day but when I came out through the gates, I realized something was wrong. Dad was there and he was shouting and yelling. I didn't know what about. I didn't really hear what he was saying. All my friends were there, staring, and I was embarrassed. I always played the class clown at school because I was so desperate to be liked but I knew even I couldn't make this funny.

I hurried over to Mum's car and got in the back seat with Ellis. She started to pull away but Dad jumped into a white van and parked it in the middle of the road so that it was blocking the way. He wound the window down. He was still shouting and yelling.

The mum of one of my friends walked past and smiled sympathetically at us, looking worried. 'Are you all right, Emma?' she asked my Mum. Mum waved at her and put on a brave smile, said she was fine. My Dad thought she was smiling at him. He thought, he would tell her later when he had her locked in the car, that she was mocking him. Dad was all about respect and now he was telling himself he was being disrespected.

Dad had to move the van in the end because he was blocking

other parents in, too, and so Mum managed to inch our car past him and we set off for my Nan's house, where we were staying while Mum waited for the council to find a new place for us. My Dad followed us in the van. He wasn't discreet about it. He sat right on our back bumper the whole way. He liked to intimidate people.

I don't know how long that journey took. Half an hour, maybe. The traffic wasn't great. It seemed like an age to me, with Dad harassing us the whole way, Mum stressed and frightened. Like I said, Dad was unpredictable.

I felt relieved when we finally pulled into Lyttleton Road. Stupid, really, because it wasn't going to affect Dad's mood but I always felt safe in Lyttleton Road. There were goalposts in the back garden and a little pond with goldfish. There was even a greenhouse where my Granddad grew tomatoes. Those tomatoes were things of wonder to me.

And my Uncle, he had his own room with a double bed in it and lots of toys. He had Super Nintendo and he had wrestlers. Ellis and I slept in a small room in our flat in Keble House in bunk beds, but my cousin had this massive room. It felt like paradise to me there. It was the only place that made me feel like that.

I used to go round and stay there on Friday nights every week so my Nan would go shopping on Thursdays and stock up. We used to get Aldi's own-brand KitKats and Aldi-brand everything at home, but my Nan always bought the real thing. That was such a thrill, eating a real KitKat, going to my Nan's, being a kid, playing outside with the other kids.

There was a Catholic church almost opposite my Nan's house called Corpus Christi and I went to the primary school that was attached to it for a short time when I was younger. There is a small patch of grass outside it that felt as big as Wembley to me and on summer evenings, we'd climb over the railings and kick a ball around until the priest came out and shooed us away.

I glanced over at the church as we pulled up outside my Nan's. Things happened fast. My Dad leaped out of the white van and ran over to our car and flung the doors open. He grabbed me and my brother and sister and marched us over to the van and locked us inside it. All we could do then was stare out of the windows at what was unfolding.

My Mum told me some of the rest. My Dad jumped into the passenger seat and slammed the car door shut. He started threatening her. 'You think you're clever, do you?' he said. 'Giving it the big one outside school, chatting to your friend and laughing at me. You think that makes you smart, do you?'

Mum said she hadn't been laughing at him. She explained that she had been trying to reassure the other mum that we were okay even though he was yelling and screaming – that she had been smiling at the woman, not at Dad. She told him she was frightened to death outside the school, not knowing what he was going to do. She said she was frightened now.

Dad put his thumbs in the corners of her mouth and started pulling them in opposite directions so that it stretched her face. 'If you want to smile, I'll give you a fucking smile,' he said. 'I'll give you a permanent smile, if you want. You can have a Joker's smile.' Then he got hold of her head and slammed it against the car window.

At that point, I saw my Mum's brother, Uncle David, come out of the house – he must have heard the commotion. He went round to the passenger-side door and remonstrated with my Dad and told him to stop hitting Mum. Dad didn't take kindly to that. He got out of the car and fronted up to Uncle David in the street and told him they were the same size so they ought to have it out.

I saw them shouting at each other for a bit. Uncle David said he didn't want to fight him and he got my Mum and walked her towards the house. It was a traumatic time for all of us. Those days and weeks were a slow nightmare. Not long after the initial incident, Dad came back to my Nan's while we were all out at school. He and Mum had had a disagreement on the phone and he wanted to come round and settle it. The front door was open and he walked in. He accused Mum of 'giving it' on the phone, being cheeky, being disrespectful. She said she was allowed an opinion. He pinned her on the stairs and put both his thumbs on her throat so that she couldn't breathe. She flailed around and tried to call for help but she couldn't get any words out. And then suddenly, he let go and walked out of the door. The next time he called, it was as if nothing had happened.

We stayed at my Nan's for a few more months, trying to come to terms with what had happened, getting on with our lives. Things settled down a little bit but Mum was frightened, obviously, about whether my Dad might attack her again. The council knew she was a single mum with three kids and they allocated us a new home after a while and we moved into a maisonette on Arbor Way, about a mile away from our old flat in Keble House.

Mum was terrified that Dad would find out where we were living. We kept it a secret as best we could and let friends know what the situation was in case he started asking around. We saw him now and again but never at our new place. Now and again, he would turn up at my Nan's in Lyttleton Road, asking where we were. She never told him.

About six months after Mum and Dad had split up, she went out on a date with someone else. I stayed over at my Nan's with Ellis and Sasha and at some point in the evening, Dad came round and asked where Mum was. He came back again around 10pm. My Nan told him again that Mum wasn't back yet. 'She's an adult, Paul,' she said to him. 'She hasn't got a curfew.'

The next day, he came back again. This time, he was in a taxi. He was acting strangely. I think he had taken some pills or something. He loaded the three of us into the back. He had somehow managed to find out where we were living in Chelmsley Wood. Mum had drilled it into us never to tell him, but he had found out.

Dad was behaving aggressively towards the taxi driver. He was wired, like he was hopped up on something. He was lying on the back seat, booting the back window. The driver looked really intimidated and alarmed. He was panicking. Dad was barking directions at him. Soon enough, we pulled up outside our flat and Dad took us up to the front door and knocked on it.

Mum opened the door quite casually and then I saw her expression turn to pure fear. I will never forget that look on my Mum's face. He burst past her into the maisonette and shoved Sasha, who was about 18 months old by then, into the living room. Then he started going from room to room, all through the flat.

'Who are you looking for?' my Mum said.

'Who were you with last night?' he asked. 'Have you spent the night on your own?'

'Yeah, I have,' Mum said.

'You're a liar,' he shouted. He started calling Mum all the names under the sun. I was crying my eyes out by now. So were Ellis and Sasha. I told him to calm down but he was out of control.

'I'm going to kill your Mum,' he said to me, and started to point at each of us kids in turn. 'And then I'm going to kill you and I'm going to kill you and I'm going to kill you.'

He began flinging punches at my Mum. I jumped up and tried to get between them and he punched me and knocked me over and hit Mum again. I got up and he punched me again. I got up and he punched me again. He said to my Mum that she had to take him back. Every time she said no, he hit her. I was jumping up and getting in front and saying, 'Don't hit my Mum' and then he'd hit me.

I just remember not staying down, getting up, getting back in front, getting up, getting back in front. That seemed to go on for ever. He picked Sasha up and flung her on a chair. Mum was trying to reason with him and reassuring us that she was okay. It was mayhem.

And then there was a knock on the door. That saved us. It was a friend of mine, Lee Millward, who lived nearby. Dad let Mum answer the door, but he was holding on to her hair to stop her running away.

'Hello, Emma,' Lee said. 'Is Troy coming out?'

'No, he fucking isn't,' my Dad said.

Lee started crying. There was a woman out in her garden next door and she asked what the matter was. Maybe she'd heard some of the commotion from inside, too, but she called the police.

They arrived quickly. They knocked on the front door and then one of the policemen pushed the door ajar. My Dad rushed over to it and slammed the door on his arm. Then he slammed it repeatedly against this arm. I don't know if he broke the guy's arm but it soon disappeared from view.

By this point, it felt as if we were hostages. The police were outside and they called for back-up. I know that because within a few minutes, loads of police vehicles pulled up outside. There were two riot vans and four police cars, all for my Dad. They forced their way in this time and wrestled him to the floor. After they had subdued him, I heard him calling me to come outside. I came out into the passageway and he was under the stairs and there were black uniforms everywhere. There were loads of them.

'Look at what these bastards have done to your Dad,' he was saying. 'All I wanted to do was see you.' I don't know whether the drugs had worn off but he seemed different and more rational suddenly. My Mum brought me back in and I saw all these riot vans pull away. I was sent to a neighbour's house to play. And then the social workers arrived. I've blacked everything else out.

I'd done the best I could but I wish I'd been bigger. In a weird way, Mum and I have got a connection from what happened. She loves all of us the same. That's without question. But we have been through hell together and that is in the back of our heads. My sister gets the best treatment because she's the only girl. Ellis was good at everything athletically, Sasha was the only girl and then there is Joel, who everyone would say is my stepbrother, and he is white.

We used to take the mickey out of him and call him the Limited Edition. You know when a chocolate bar puts a white chocolate bar out just for a little while. My thing is I'm the oldest plus we have been through all that shit. My Mum's now in her mid-fifties and my Dad's dead. They never got back together. It took years but she's genuinely happy now. She's got married.

Mum talked about the trauma of that incident recently. 'I don't think he would have hurt any of us more than he already had,' she said, 'but if the police hadn't come, it would have been mind games the whole time. Threats. What he was going to do. The threats to hurt me were usually against you. Because you were mine. I told him I hadn't had to share you with him but I chose to.

'When he wanted to get at me, it would be Troy that took the brunt of it. In the past, when he had hit me, or the time he strangled me, I hadn't pressed charges. But this time I wasn't going to let it go. Because he had hit Troy. He had assaulted a child. Troy had meetings with the social worker every second Saturday for six months and Paul went to jail for nine weeks for what he did to us.'

So my Dad went to jail, Mum was black and blue and I was seeing a social worker. And no one spoke about any of it. It was an end of innocence for me. I started identifying being at my Nan's with that horror story. Before, it had been the fun stuff. Now it was a place that was associated with a lot of unhappy things. Nan and Granddad moved when I was about 13. I was gutted when they left. It was the last Holy Grail of nice places and by that point we were on house number four. We just kept moving.

It destroyed my relationship with my Dad for a few years. I forgave him for it, but I never forgot. It made a huge impact on me. A few days after the beating at Arbor Road, I went to school and someone tripped me over, as kids do, trying to be funny. I thought, *No one will ever do that to me again, no one will ever bully me.* I just whacked the kid with my hand.

I had that moment where I looked at my hand after I had hit him and thought, *That works.* I will not let people think I am weak. Maybe I don't mean weak, because we're all weak. I won't let it fester. I won't let people build up the courage to think they can attack me. I'll ask if they have a problem and diffuse it that way.

I didn't learn those lessons for free. My teeth are all jagged from the moment when my Dad hit me. They were all misaligned from it and that is why I will never get my teeth done. It reminds me every day. Maybe I need to be reminded of it for balance. I am very fortunate. I live in a beautiful home, which I have managed to pay for. My kids all go to private school. My Mum and my brothers and sister are all healthy. I need balance.

I struggled with love for a very long time, with understanding what love is, how to be okay. I shouldered all responsibility for a long time. So these are reminders that things can happen. Look where you have come from and what you have overcome and don't get too confident that this can't be taken away from you very quickly.

After the beating in Arbor Way, we tried to get back to normal as best we could. I was back at school and everyone was tip-toeing around me. I felt like I was being made to stand out in a way I didn't want to stand out. I had the idea that the teachers and the other kids were feeling sorry for me and I hated that.

A couple of months later, we were out with Mum in her car and we stopped at the petrol station in Chelmsley Wood. A bus pulled up across the road and it caught my eye for some reason. When it pulled away, my Dad was standing there alone. It made my heart leap. I wondered if there was going to be more trouble.

He was carrying a big see-through plastic bag full of clothes. He'd been released from prison that day. He'd served his punishment for what he did to us, at least in the eyes of the law. He shouted over to my Mum and asked if the kids were in the car. She nodded and he wandered over. 'I'm not going to do anything,' he said. He'd probably seen the fear in our faces. He actually asked her if we could give him a lift back to his place and she agreed.

She told me later that she agreed so that it would feel normal to us. Part of her had wanted to run to the car as soon as she saw him get off the bus, slam the door and drive off as fast as she could. But she knew that would have made us scared and all she ever wanted to do was protect us. I think she had a sense that my Dad wasn't going to attack us again. So she tried to make us think everything was normal. He came round to the passenger door and told me to get in the back seat and that was it.

I'd never been scared of him before. Not until he beat me up. After that, I was petrified of him for a long time. Why would you do that to me? That was the feeling I had. I still struggle with that to this day. I can't stand bullies. I was nine or ten. I had no chance of beating a grown man in a fight. Over the years, we got closer and if he hadn't died so young, I think we would have built a really strong relationship, but back then, I was scared stiff. The first time he came round to our house after he had beaten us up, I didn't know he was coming. I walked into the kitchen and he was there. I pissed myself because I was so frightened. I remember looking down at my trousers and thinking, *What the fuck?* I had no control over it. I pissed myself. That killed him. He kept saying, 'It's okay, I'm not going to touch you.' He was about ten yards away. He said he just wanted to say hello and give me a hug. But I pissed myself, I was that scared of him.

A year or so later, I was chasing some kid around the estate because we'd had an argument and he climbed up on to a shed. I thought I could clamber up and get him but as I was pulling myself up on to the roof, he turned around and kicked me in the face and I went flying backwards off the top of the shed and landed hard on my elbow. I looked at it and it was a big ball of blood.

I ran home and told Mum what had happened. She said she was going out. It was going to be her first night out since my Dad had attacked us and she said she wasn't going to ruin it just because I had a scratch on my elbow. She was adamant. She had a look at it and softened a bit, but she knew I was a hypochondriac and she said if she took me to the hospital and there was nothing wrong, I'd owe her big time. We got there and the nurse on reception at A&E said I needed to go straight to X-ray. I was in a hospital bed in half an hour and I could see the guilt written all over Mum's face straight away.

I was in hospital for a week with my arm elevated and every day and night and every time I woke up my Dad was sitting in the chair by my bed. He was there with me constantly, looking after me, keeping me company. All of the other stuff had gone at that point because when I needed him the most, he was there next to me. It was a strange dynamic. It's probably why I'm so messed up now.

CHAPTER 4

DON'T BACK OUT

I've told you all these stories about what my Dad was capable of but there's a contradiction at the heart of all it: despite everything, he was still my superhero. The violence is bound to be the headline act in a young life but those incidents were isolated events. For the vast majority of the time, he was a loving Dad who looked after me and my siblings and made me feel safe.

He was a huge influence on me. A tombstone is tattooed on my right arm and the stone bears the name Paul Anthony Burke. It records the dates of his birth and death. Lower down the arm are images that depict his battles with light and darkness and higher up, guarded by an angel, is an imagining of the gates of heaven where I hope my Dad is now at peace.

He was cool. He was just a cool individual. He was funny. He was someone you wanted to be around and he had unbelievable street credibility in our area. The problem was as soon as he had a drink or drugs, he turned into someone completely different. When he and my Mum used to go out, she enjoyed it until he had a drink and then he was a ticking time bomb.

But he put us in a position where we could make something of ourselves. If he hadn't had me playing with a football at six, who knows? I might not have been into football at all. I might never have got to this level. I might never have been able to make this life for myself. I might have glorified what he did and gone down that route. In many ways, I am reaping the benefits of the hard work he did.

The truth is, he made us petrified about what would happen if he suspected we were trying to follow the path he had gone down. He said if he ever saw any of us trying to be a gangster, he would go to town on us. Actually, I wanted to be a firefighter. We have a family friend who was a firefighter but he did lots of jobs for my Nan. I knew he did four days on and four days off so I thought if I was a firefighter, I could sleep for four days.

When my Dad wasn't drinking or smoking, he was happy-go-lucky. When you with that version of Dad, you felt like you were in the safest place in the world. It's probably how we want our kids to feel when they are around us. You just don't want them to see your angry side. And I saw my Dad's angry side, big time. I don't think it was the real him but it still can't unsee what I saw.

I was a bit wary of him for several years after the incident at Arbor Way. I knew he loved me but there was always the memory of what he had done to me and the lingering question of 'What would stop you doing it again?' That's really harsh because I'm the perfect example of making a mistake and trying to change my life in the aftermath of it.

Throughout my teens, I wouldn't say we were close. I felt like he was closer to my brother and sister because their memory of the earlier situation was a little bit different. Their age protected them a little bit from the memory of what had happened. I could feel that 5 per cent deficit of trust that my brother and sister didn't have.

Then, as I said, when I got to my mid-teens, I got curious about meeting my biological father and Mum arranged that I would spend a day with him. I felt like that broke my Dad as well. I felt bad for him. In hindsight, I wish I hadn't done that. I feel like I betrayed him at that point because when I was a child and Colin Hemmings deserted us, Dad was the one who picked up the slack and took me on.

The meeting with Colin Hemmings was a waste of time, as I said earlier. I felt like I was a prize pig when I arrived at his home. 'Troy's here, guys,' he said. It was like a Mexican stand-off of bemusement between me and the other relatives who were there. I didn't know them. They didn't know me. Within a couple of hours, I had messaged my Mum and asked her to come and get me.

I never spoke with my Dad about it but I knew he knew I'd been to visit. When Mum picked me up from Colin Hemmings' house, she asked if I was all right and I said, 'He's a fucking arsehole, don't ever let me do that again.' That was the last time I ever spoke about him or asked about him. It was done. It was finished. It was clarification that he was what everyone said he was.

My Dad wasn't a bad man. It was circumstance. He had a tough upbringing as well. He was from an old-school Jamaican family.

He ran away with the circus when he was six or seven and grew up in inner-city England at a time when racism was rife and there were National Front marches and all the rest of it.

My Nan and Granddad were part of the Windrush generation and they were happy here, working and providing for their family, but my Dad didn't like the rules. He just got into a certain lifestyle from an early age which was productive for him. It's a bit like I was with drinking: when people told me to stop drinking because it would affect my football, I told them I was getting drunk and scoring hat-tricks and I was in the Premier League so what are you on about?

My Dad had a saying he used to repeat: if you don't learn, you'll feel. He would tell us once but he wouldn't tell us twice. The second time, you'd get a smack. If I did something wrong and somebody said they were going to tell my Dad, that struck fear into me.

He was quite fun and easy-going most of the time but I do remember an occasion where I dared Ellis to swear at him and say, 'Dad, you're shit.' Ellis was five. He went into the other room where Dad was sitting and he did it because he was game for anything. I heard a smack across the legs and I was laughing and then he shouted my name. Uh-oh.

He took us both into the bathroom and he got a bar of the old Imperial Leather soap that had the little piece of paper on the top and he said, 'Both of you, wash your mouths out.' We were putting it in our mouths as gently as we could and then he whacked it and rammed it into our mouths and the bars of soap were ingrained with our teeth marks all the way through. I would never do that to my kids obviously but those were the times. You respected your elders and called your friends' parents 'Mr' or 'Mrs' until they told you it wasn't necessary.

The first meeting with my Dad after he attacked us at Arbor Way was in an office with a social worker present. We went through a door into a back garden and my Dad was sitting there at one of the tables having a fag. My brother and sister went running over to see him as if nothing had happened and I just kind of wandered over. The social worker kept saying, 'I'm here if you need me.' I felt like I was being mothered a little bit, just not by the right person. I was just numb. I didn't feel like I'd missed him. I didn't feel like I hated him. I just felt numb.

At school, I became this victim and I hated it. Because Dad had hit me and my Mum, he wasn't allowed near the school. My Mum had had to inform the school about it and everyone in the area knew anyway. There was a meeting with the social worker, my teacher Mr Henry, myself and the headmaster, Mr Hemery, and my Mum. I remember being there but it was as if everyone was talking over my head.

They were discussing coping strategies for dealing with Dad. 'If he comes, we need to do this…' – all that kind of stuff. There was this fear factor that he might come back. Mum knew what he was like. It didn't matter if there was an injunction or something like that against him. He didn't give a damn. Unless there was a physical barrier stopping him from what he wanted to do, he was going to do it.

After that, every session at school was like 'Troy, are you okay?' I'd say, 'Yeah, why?' I'm a kid. I'd forgotten about it really. Because no one in my family really spoke about it. And so I thought, *Why would I speak about it?* I had my brother and sister and as long as we protected them, I was all right. It was a different generation. Kids were to be seen and not heard.

In school, there was me and a girl called Kirsty and she was diabetic so she used to get crisps in lessons. And we'd complain because she got crisps and we didn't. And after the incident happened, I felt like Kirsty. I felt like people were saying, 'Why has Troy got a teacher sat next to him, why is he getting extra help?' I felt like the dummy of the school. I felt like I was being babied, like people were watching me to see how much damage there was. I went through a phase where I blacked out a lot of stuff from the age of ten to fifteen.

My family is Jamaican and Irish and no one talked about stuff on either side. You didn't tell anyone your problems. You didn't want to feel like a victim. You didn't want anyone to feel pity. You would get on with things. As long as your dirty laundry stayed indoors, it didn't matter.

Now, there are so many avenues for people to talk. I don't recall ever knowing the full truth about my Dad until I buried him when I was 21 or 22 and that was only by asking questions and people reminiscing. A lot of the stories were variations on a theme of 'There was this time when your Dad did this or that to somebody.'

The fact that I wasn't his biological son and that he took stuff out on me because of that is something that I talk about a lot in therapy.

It's a huge part of why I want to be liked. We all want to be liked but more so in my case. It was only in negative times that those things came up with my Dad so it was not as if I felt isolated or ostracized as a matter of course.

I just knew if there was an argument or if something went wrong or someone had to miss out, then I would be the one who missed out. I was cool with it but it lodged with me and it has come out tenfold as I have got older. I do things to be liked. I am desperate to be loved, I suppose. I feel my brother and sister have always been put above me and I do it, too. I put them above me.

If someone tells me I'm the successful one, I say, 'My sister Sasha's the smart one of the family' and she is. If they say I'm a great footballer, I tell them, 'My brother Ellis is so much better than me' and I genuinely believe that. I just got lucky. The feeling of them being placed higher in the pecking order than me by family doesn't stem from anything they did intentionally. It was subconscious. It was in the background. At least, that was how it seemed to me. My understanding of our childhood, compared to my brother and sister's, would be completely different.

I was angry about parts of my childhood. I'm still angry now. I'm envious. I'm envious of people that have happy relationships with their parents. When you see that family walking down the road and it's the mum, dad and the kids all walking the dog, I get jealous of that. It was never an option for me with my biological father but it was taken away from me with my Dad when he died young.

It hurts. It goes back to my sense of not being good enough. I know logically I had absolutely nothing to do with any of it, but it doesn't change the feeling. I didn't do anything wrong but I paid a price.

It even extended to football. Because Ellis was so good at football, even if I won man of the match, I was never the best in my team. I was never the main player. Ellis was the main player in his team. So I might be man of the match but Ellis would have scored four goals the same week. I was doing it at Sunday league level but Ellis was on the books at Aston Villa from a young age. I might have played well against a team from Solihull. Ellis had just played really well against Manchester United.

My Granddad was a diehard Villa fan so whatever Ellis had done was better. He would talk about Ellis all the time. It wasn't meant to come out that way. 'Troy, did you see Ellis did this?' Sometimes, I felt like saying, 'Hi, I'm here as well!' From the age of 12, I took the back seat and I had to pick Ellis and Sasha up from school and then my football and my interests came second and third behind theirs.

Ellis got picked up by Villa from the age of six until he was 20 or 21 so he was the favourite by default. He was all of our favourites. He was the great hope, I suppose. New life all lent on his shoulders and we were all going to have a better life because of what Ellis could do. I helped out with that. I was an enabler. I was 11 when I had my first job, helping my Mum clean the bookies. I did glass collecting in the pubs. When my Mum was working, I would pick the kids up from school.

Ellis had training on a Tuesday for Villa and it was a military operation for all of us. We had to have had tea and be waiting so that when Mum pulled up in the car after work, we dashed out and got straight into Mum's car to take Ellis to the football. It could take us up to an hour sometimes with traffic.

We'd get there, I'd watch the football and follow what they were learning. I would try and get it right so that if Ellis needed to practise in the garden, I could do it with him.

Sundays were about going to watch Ellis's game. There were a couple of dads there that were quite nice to me. I fell into the role of the supportive one to my younger, more talented brother.

Ellis was mustard. He was left-footed. He had the same broad shoulders when he was seven as he has now. He is built like a triangle. He is massive. He had a good football brain, too. In fact, he had a good brain altogether. You could show him a laptop and he's never seen it before and he'll be working it better than you by the end of the day. Give him rollerblades and he'll be going backwards in half an hour. He comes round and fixes stuff. He is a proper doer.

He was the best athlete I'd ever seen. He played left wing for Villa and I watched a game against Man United and he scored and even the Man United guy asked my Dad who Ellis was. My Dad was so loud and he was going round telling everyone, 'Man United want my son now.' I don't think Ellis ever took any of it as pressure. Even now, he is happy-go-lucky.

I don't know how he dealt with it, though. Even when he went round to my Granddad's, Granddad would be peppering him with questions about Villa and Graham Taylor. There was this expectation that he was going to be Ronaldo. He had a lot more pressure than me. It's funny the way it's transpired really. I could develop out of the spotlight. I wouldn't have been mentally prepared for anything more at that age.

As long as I could play football and my pals thought I was decent, that was my enough for me. We had Monday night football. My best friend at school ran the team and all of the cool kids from our area played in his team and I could play centre midfield for them so I thought I was the man then. That was my aspiration.

I found out where Chelmsley Town played and a lot of the lads who played for them were local men who could handle themselves. They were somebodys in our area. So when I was 15, I wanted to play for Chelmsley Town. If I could play for Chelmsley Town, then I was the man. If I could show them that I was good enough to play for them, they would at least let me hang around with them.

That was all I wanted. That was how my mind worked. I just wanted people to like me. As long as somebody likes me, I'll be all right and that was it.

I have fond memories of our childhood. I like looking back to secondary school. I had some good mates. School was like a playground for me all the time. I thought school was easy. Once I figured out that all the answers were in the book, I thought it was a waste of time. I just wanted to make people laugh and be socially accepted.

I sometimes went to extreme lengths to achieve that. In Year 7, we were all given a book that had three pages at the back that were marked with slots for detentions. I told everyone I had made up my mind I would fill all those pages up with detentions until I ran out of slots and I made good on that promise. I thought that would make me cool.

I suppose it really ought not have been a surprise when they threatened to kick me out in Year 10 but my sports teacher intervened on my behalf and persuaded them to give me a reprieve. I was more of an annoyance than a bad kid. I didn't take my GCSEs. I did two exams, put my name on the paper and fell asleep. And that was it. I just left.

I got into building college because my cousin Joe Burke was doing it. He was a cool kid, he was popular with the girls and they were going to pay me £80 a week to do it, so I followed him. We never had money and so money was never spoken about. I thought if you had a job, you had your own house. If someone had a legal job, they owned a house. If you didn't have a legal job, you lived in a council house.

My football journey began at the 3Cs really. There were two teams in Chelmsley Wood: the 3Cs and Chelmsley Town. I played for the 3Cs for a long time, throughout my junior career. We were the best team in Chelmsley and may even have been the best team in Birmingham. Some of our lads went to play for Blues, Villa, Derby. We were so good it was surreal.

I did okay. I had people from league clubs looking at me but I was never the one that shone. I was never the big kid. I was never the fast kid. I was never the one with the most powerful shot – but I was decent. I started off as a centre-half as a kid. Then I ended up in midfield. Until I went to Walsall, I played centre midfield.

I enjoy scoring but it's not the be-all and end-all. You know how some strikers could lose 8–1 and as long as they score the one, they're okay. I prefer to win. That comes from wanting to be a midfielder and wanting to play a good pass and see the game differently.

The 3Cs didn't have an adults' team, which was one reason why I thought about leaving and I was also aware that a lot of the cool people played for Chelmsley Town. The other thing about the 3Cs was that I had got bored of winning. I didn't really feel there was a challenge. I thought Chelmsley Town would be a laugh so I played a year for the Under-16s and then went into men's football.

My best mate Marc Williams, who has always been known as Disk, was playing for them. My cousin Joe was there, too, and he was a big influence on me. There was a social element attached to it as well. The Chelmsley Town boys would play on Saturday afternoon, have a beer afterwards and then go out into Birmingham. I liked the idea of belonging.

The senior team at Chelmsley was in the Midland Combination 2. God knows how many tiers down that is. Eleven or twelve, I think. There was a glitch at the start because I couldn't afford to pay my subs for about the first six months and it got to a point where Chelmsley Town said they weren't going to let me play. The 3Cs cut me a bit of slack because they knew my Mum and they knew what we had gone through but it was different at Chelmsley Town and they tried to bar me from the clubhouse. In the end, my cousin Joe paid it.

I came across a piece on the club website the other day that recorded my first weeks with them. It mentioned my reserve team debut away at Cresonians in September 2004, where I scored in a 5–0 victory. After what is reported as a 'spectacular display' at Mile Oak Rovers, Chelmsley Town were short on numbers and the gaffer, Steve Solomon, gave me his own number 8 shirt for my first team debut. According to the report, I was 'one of the most valuable members of the first team squad ever since'.

So I was 16 and playing men's football. It was an education. We'd meet at McDonald's at 9.30am, leave at 9.40am and kick off was 10.30am I saw the lads arriving. Disk turned up at 9.42am in his black Megane. I asked if I could get in his car and he started telling me about the fight he'd had the night before. Welcome to men's football.

There were some good teams in that league. One of our opponents was Birmingham Police and they played on immaculate pitches in Edgbaston. Also, you were playing against a copper so you would always leave a bit on them or they would leave a bit on you. They could definitely handle themselves. Chelmsley Wood has got a bit of a reputation so there was a bit more spice to it.

We had a few lads who were going for a ruck and were going to play right on the edge of what is fair and not fair. Playing at 16 in that kind of football is what has enabled me to get through all of this because it was brutal at times and I was playing with some serious individuals.

It was carnage. That was my football upbringing. If you backed out of a tackle, they would let you know. 'Don't fucking embarrass us.' I played against Cadbury Town and they had a pitch right next to Cadbury World that was beautiful. I was chasing down the goalie and I heard them shouting, 'Don't back out.' It was a short ball and the keeper was coming to me and I was running towards him. I went in full-blooded and won the ball and heard a big crack.

The ball ran loose and I slid it into the empty net. I turned round and I saw the lad on the ground and I realized straight away I had broken this keeper's leg. Maybe now you would slide or slow down a bit but back then it was full force. There was no scrap or anything. There were no complaints from Cadbury Town. It was a fair tackle. We stood around for half an hour, waiting for the ambulance to come. Then he was put on a stretcher and loaded into the ambulance and the game restarted.

I soon realized I was playing with some serious individuals. There were lads from some of the rough parts of Birmingham: Newtown, Nechells, Erdington. I couldn't drive so I was grabbing lifts with them and hearing some of the things that were being said and thinking, *What am I doing with these people?* Some guy was on trial for attempted murder and the other lads were asking him when he was due back in court. I just saw him as a really nice bloke. I think they saw me as the kid who would do all their running for them.

I didn't think it was going to lead to anything. Not a chance. I was a bricklayer by then and I thought that would probably be my future. I helped to build the doctors' surgery in Chelmsley Wood actually and it's still there. Maybe I missed my vocation.

CHAPTER 5
DICKIE DOSH

When I was 17, playing football as a professional wasn't in my path. I played football because I loved the game but doing it for a living was never my dream. It was my brother's dream. We were going to make sure Ellis was perfect and when he was perfect, he would look after the rest of us. He would take care of us. He would be our ticket out. We devoted everything we could to giving him the best platform.

It never quite worked out for him at Villa in the end. Maybe we put too much pressure on him. Maybe he felt the weight of all our dreams. He has had a good career in non-league football with clubs like Kettering Town, Worcester City, Tamworth and Telford United. He has got all the talent but he never got the breaks he needed. The death of our Dad hit him very hard because Dad was the one that pushed him and gave him the framework for his football.

Because of Ellis, I was allowed to fly under the radar. No one expected anything of me so I didn't really take football too seriously. I just played it to enjoy it. I had a week's trial at Villa when I was 15 or 16 and I turned up for the first day and then spent the next three days hanging out with my mates and chasing girls in the park.

I knew that there was a practice match on the last day of the trial and so I figured that as long as I turned up for that, that would be when the decision would be made about who they might offer an apprenticeship to. That wasn't quite how Villa approached it, unfortunately. They saw that I hadn't turned up for three days and after the practice match, they told me I wasn't going to be invited back.

I wasn't too bothered. I didn't expect anything anyway. Why would Villa want to sign someone like me? I started playing for Chelmsley Town and working as a bricklayer and that was enough for me. I was happy with that. I was playing with cool guys and that made me a cool guy. But then fate intervened.

I went out with the lads on a Friday night as normal. I was a bit the worse for wear the next morning but Mum got me up and kicked me out of the house so she could do some cleaning. So I went and played for Chelmsley Town. I scored four goals that day and it turned out that Walsall's chief scout, Mick Halsall, was watching the game.

He had only come to the game because his son was playing and because the match he was supposed to have been watching had been called off. He came up to me in the pub afterwards and asked if I'd be interested in having a try-out with Walsall. I didn't really care, to be honest. It wasn't as if it was some amazing moment for me.

To me, he's just an old man asking me a question in a pub. I told him I didn't even know where Walsall was. It was about 20 minutes from my house but I'd barely been outside Chelmsley Wood at that stage of my life. He persisted. He told me to come in on Monday for a one-week trial. I shrugged it off, really. I didn't want to commit to it. I didn't really want to commit to anything at that age.

He didn't have to take the time. Nothing in his life has changed by improving my life, but he saw something. He saw what I could become. I always give him so much credit – he changed my life – but whenever I tell him that, he denies it. 'No,' he says, 'all I did was give you an opportunity. The rest you did yourself.' I needed an intervention, though, and Mick provided it.

I never had ambition because I had never seen ambition. Everyone who went to my school ended up working at Land Rover or the Dunlop factory. They still lived at home, they could pay their mum rent and keep and go out on the weekend. They were the ones I could identify with. I would always get picked in a football team but I was never 'the one'. I knew where the top kids were. But with me, you don't have to open the door and show me everything. You just have to crack the seal and say, 'If you just get through that, the opportunities are endless.'

I went out that Saturday night, as you do. I went out Sunday night, too. It wasn't as if I had anything else to do. The bricklaying job I had been doing had finished and so I was effectively unemployed. And then at nine o'clock on Monday morning, I'm lying in bed and someone starts knocking on the door. It was Derek Brennan, Chairman of Chelmsley Town. He said he had come to give me a lift to Walsall.

I jumped out of bed and because I'd played Sunday league the day before, my boots were all caked in mud. I put them in an Asda bag and flung on a track suit, jumped in the car and off we went. We got to the Bescot Stadium and Derek dropped me off. I asked him how I was going to get home but he told me I was on my own now.

When I first walked through the door, it was intimidating. The best level of football I had seen up to that point was my brother training with the kids at Villa. It was still part-time and still amateurish. They got beans on toast and a drink to go home with and I thought that was professionalism. This was different. Walsall might have been in League Two and the surroundings might have been humble but training was serious.

I didn't get any proper kit. Someone took me to lost property, picked out a pair of shorts with the number 87 on them and gave me a top with the number 6, which was a couple of sizes too big. It was a new world. I went to the away changing room where the young lads changed in those days and there were a few Scousers there. I had never met a Scouser. I wondered how they had got there.

I was introduced to the other lads. There was a kid called Manny Smith who was from my area and we were a bit stand-offish because of our outside alliances, shall we say. There was this wild kid called Ishmel Demontagnac, from London, and he was loud and arrogant. Very cocksure. He did things on his own time and I thought, *Who's this prick?* I didn't really speak to anyone because I was so uncomfortable. After a while, however, I did get on really well with both Manny and Ishmel.

There was a lad called Alex Nicholls and he frustrated me. Chelsea had taken him on trial from Walsall and he always thought he was better than he was. He had nice stuff on, he was from Stourbridge, which was a nice area of Birmingham, the area Jude Bellingham comes from. He was one of those lads who walked with his chest puffed out like he was incredibly pleased with himself. I thought he looked down on me. I thought I'd love to smash his face in.

My first game was for the Under-18s and I nearly ended my career in the first ten seconds. I was so excited. I jumped for a ball with the opposition keeper, headed both the ball and the keeper, jumped up and nearly passed out. The first-team manager, Richard Money, was at the game and I scored and assisted and we won 2–0.

My Granddad had given me a lift to that game in his black taxi so I arrived there looking like someone out of *Shameless*. Richard Money walked past when I was leaving the ground and my Granddad, who had a stutter and was shy about talking in public, shouted out: 'Are you going to give him a fucking contract or what?' Money smiled.

It was a good question, though. There didn't seem to be much prospect of a contract, even after I'd come through that initial one-week trial. They didn't offer me a full contract at that point, but they did extend my trial for a few weeks more. I was getting my travel expenses paid but that was about it. I was borrowing money from my Mum and those close to me most of the time.

I was playing in reserve games and scoring and so, after a little while, Walsall sent me out on loan to Halesowen Town, who played in the Southern League Premier Division.

I couldn't afford to go there and play for nothing. I had just bought some white Nike boots for £85 out of my Nan's catalogue and it was £1.36 a week to pay it back to my Nan so that was my first target. I scored in my first game for Halesowen and when I went back to the clubhouse after the match to get some food, I saw the other players in there getting handed brown envelopes.

I asked one of them what it was and he said wages. The deal was you went in to the clubhouse to speak to the fans and then you got your cash. There was a goal bonus and this kid I was talking to pulled out £400 in front of me. My first thought was *rob him* and then I thought, *Why is he getting £400 and I am getting nothing for doing the same thing?*

I spoke to them and Halesowen told me I could have £50 a game and £50 a goal. That was good enough for me and I threw myself into it. We trained on a Tuesday and a Thursday and I was training at Walsall too so I was training every night of the week.

Mick Halsall used to stay out with me for ages after training, working on my touch all the time. I did really well there. I think I got eight goals in ten games. If I scored, I got the brown envelope. That was all I remembered. That was all that mattered.

I enjoyed it at Halesowen. They even had fans who travelled to away games. We played against Merthyr Tydfil in Wales and there was this bloke for Merthyr who must have been 6ft 4in and about 19 stone and he sprinted past Manny Smith and beat him to the ball. We were 2–0 down at half time and our manager, Martin O'Connor, who was a Birmingham City legend, blasted this drinks bottle everywhere.

'Manny,' he said, 'if you can't outsprint that fat bastard, you might as well quit football now.' And he turned to me – I had my brand-new white boots on and in my head I looked like Ronaldo – and said he would kick me out of the club if I didn't buck up. I thought I was going to lose that brown envelope. I scored a hat-trick in the second half but my brand new boots split and I was fuming. They gave me an extra £50 for that game.

I didn't know it when I played but it turned out that that game was a test I had to pass. Apparently, in Mick Halsall's mind there were three of us in that Halesowen team vying for a contract at Walsall and he only had one contract to give out.

The other two were better than me. I feel pretty clear in my mind about that.

So we played Merthyr Tydfil away. Halesowen had no money, so you travelled to south Wales from the Midlands by coach on the day of the match. It takes about five hours to get there. It was raining, it was horrible. We won 3–2, I scored the hat-trick. We arrived back in Walsall at 2.30am, and finally crawled into bed at about 3am or 4am.

Mick Halsall phoned up all three of us at eight the next morning and told us we had to come in for training. The other two didn't answer the phone but me, lazy Troy who once couldn't give a monkey's, I answered the phone and went in to the club. I got in at 9am and Mick said, 'You can go home now.' It was a test to see how hungry I was to make it.

In the January of that first season at Walsall, they gave me a six-month contract for £120 a week. Walsall were in League Two but we were having a good season under Richard Money. He was probably the first person who exposed me to the basic psychology of football. He had a points target for each stage of the season pinned up in the dressing room and if you hit that target, it meant you were heading for promotion.

After my loan spell ended, I started to come into contention for a place in Walsall's first team towards the end of the season when we were right in the shake-up for promotion to League One. We were top of the table at the start of April, with five or six games left to play, and I made my league debut on 7 April 2007, when we played Torquay United at Plainmoor.

I think we needed a point to be sure of promotion and we were 2–1 up with about ten minutes to go when Richard Money told me to get ready to come on. 'If you stop running for one second,' he said, 'you will never play again in your career. Wherever the ball goes, fucking chase it.' I came on for Martin Butler in the 84th minute and whether their left-back had it or their right-back or their centre-forward, I ran and ran and ran and I chased and chased and chased.

We saw the game out and when I got on the bus later, Richard Money said, 'You'll do for me, son, now go and make me a cup of coffee.' And then for the next hour, I was making all the microwave meals for the rest of the lads. That was the kind of grounding it was. At the town hall presentation to celebrate promotion, they introduced me as the next Steve Bull. I didn't know who that was.

The next season, they offered me £120 a week and I bit their hand off. And so now I was a League One player. Not just a League One player, either, but a player in a really good squad. We had Clayton Ince in goal, Danny Fox at left-back, Scott Dann in defence, Ishmel Demontagnac, who went on to play in the Premier League with Blackpool, Darren Wrack and Tommy Mooney. Danny Sonner came in, too. It was ridiculous.

We started the season off and Richard Money, who the supporters had begun calling Dickie Dosh, put all the old boys in. I was on the bench most of the time. We didn't win in any of our first seven games but I was still on the bench when we went to the New Den to play Millwall on 15 September 2007. I got on for the last six minutes again with the scores level at 1–1. I scored two minutes later to win the game.

I found the old BBC report of the match. It wasn't a long one.

Troy Deeney's late strike gave Walsall victory over Millwall and lifted the side off the foot of League One. Daniel Fox gave Walsall the lead when he converted Edrissa Sonko's centre in the 41st minute.

Andrew Frampton looked to have salvaged a point for the Lions when he cleverly hooked home Neil Harris' pass from close range. Deeney grabbed the winner when he poked in Sonko's lofted cross past the dive of Rob Douglas

That was it. Fame at last.

The routine on the bus journey home was the same, though. Darren Wrack said well done on the goal and then he gave me the food order for all the players on the bus. They were all M&S ready meals. I was like the lunch lady. An hour or so afterwards, I checked they had everything before I sat back down. The senior lads told Manny to go and make some food for me and they told me to phone my Mum and tell her I'd scored my first goal in professional football. I loved all that. I think it has made me who I am today. Don't get above your station.

We had a meeting the next day and the gaffer made a big speech. 'Right,' he said, 'that's our first win, we build from here, the young lads have shown what they are about. All you old lads, if you don't want to be here, put your hand up and let me know.'

I looked round and saw Danny Sonner put his hand up. He was quite a character. He looked like a taller version of Gareth Ainsworth. He looked at Richard Money and he just said: 'Yeah, not for me, cheers, lads' and he walked out. I never saw him again.

I learned some early lessons about the reality of a football career while I was at Walsall. At the age of 34 Martin Butler had just got us promoted. He had scored a few goals and had an offer to go somewhere else. Walsall tried to stand in his way and it was the first time I saw a player kicking the ball away and sulking in training. I asked him what he was doing.

He said that when you get older, football's about money, it's not just about playing. He told me he didn't ever want to see me doing it and he hoped it never got to that point for me. He kept walking through training and in the end, he got his way. He made it so they had to get rid of him.

Then there was Alex Nicholls. My opinion of him didn't really improve that much. We got on the coach to go to an away match at Barnsley once and I was one of the last to sit down. I think Alex was a bit jealous of me because I had started to move through the ranks a bit and he hadn't.

I went to sit down next to him but he had this Louis Vuitton washbag on the seat next to him and he went 'whoa, whoa, whoa' and pointed at it and said 'That seat's taken'. On the way back, I sat in his seat and when he got on, I said, 'Your seat's back there, mate.' I didn't hate him or anything like that. He just wasn't my cup of tea. He moved on to Northampton Town and his career was effectively ended in a match against Port Vale by a disgraceful tackle that broke his leg very badly. Whatever my feelings about him, no one deserves that.

Once I was in at Walsall, I realized very quickly that you can transition from my level to making a career and a solid income by playing football. I thought, *Okay, let's give this a whirl.* That goal at Millwall was my only goal of the 2007–08 season but after Richard Money had left the club that April and Jimmy Mullen had come and gone as manager, Chris Hutchings took over and I hit a rich scoring vein.

Michael Ricketts had joined the club by then. What a player he was. He was past his prime by the time he arrived at Walsall but you could see how good he had been. He still had class as a player. He'd played for England once and for top teams like Bolton and Leeds and Middlesbrough and even though he was on the downslope of his career now, I learned a lot from him.

Ricko had all the trappings of football stardom, too. He had an apartment in Miami and a black BMW that looked like a spaceship. I was driving my Mum's Ford Focus to training at the new facility the club had built in Cannock. We would get to work at five to ten every day and if we were a bit early, we'd stop at Hilton Park Services on the M6 and get a McDonald's breakfast.

One day, he gave me his bank card and told me to get some money out of the ATM and buy some of his favourite gummy bears or whatever they were: chewy sweets that were shaped like pigs. I did what he asked and when I got back to the car, he asked me if I'd looked at the ATM receipt. I said I hadn't so he held it up. It showed his bank account had a massive amount in it. It wasn't that he was boasting. He wasn't like that. He was putting me in my place. He was telling me that if I thought I was a big shot, I had a long way to go.

In my second full season at Walsall, I often played up front with Ricko and Jabo Ibere. Ricko spent a lot of his time injured or suspended, but when he was available, he played. I'm not sure his heart was in it, really. He was too good for that level and he was frustrated about where he was. He only played on for another year after he left Walsall.

Ricko was the one who taught me how to play the position right.

Tommy Mooney told me to hit the targets, be professional, be on time. He taught me how to be a professional. I listened to Moons more than Ricko because I was more like Moons. I wasn't as good as Ricko and I knew that players like Moons and me had to run more to be successful.

Ricko made me play two-touch every day. He made me work and work and work on my technique. He was testing my touch. Ricketts was a pure baller who never quite achieved his ambitions because he didn't have the same work ethic as some other professionals and all he ate was chocolate, but he genuinely invested time in me and I'll always be grateful to him for that.

Darren Byfield arrived at Walsall, too. He was from Aston and he was a bit more my kind of guy, rough and rugged and had a bit of a chip on his shoulder. With him and Ricko, it was the first time I'd really experienced a black environment in football. For the first time, it was okay to listen to rap music before games. I liked Byfield. He played with a kind of aggression that was right on the edge.

Mooney was great with me, too. He was getting on a bit and before we signed him, Richard Money had made me travel to Wycombe away and write a full-page report on him. I didn't know we were about to sign him.

He was in his mid-30s by then and I wrote in my report about what great movement he had but that he was a bit slow and looked like he was carrying a few pounds. We signed him a few weeks later and Dickie Dosh showed him what I'd written about him. Moons said as long as I was that honest with him face to face, we'd get on.

Maybe the biggest character of all of the players in that Walsall team was Anthony Gerrard, who went on to play for Cardiff City in the League Cup final. Gez is a lovely human being but he is also a lunatic. We got into a cycle of playing practical jokes on each other at Walsall, which is not uncommon in football dressing rooms, but when Gez got involved, it quickly spiralled out of control.

It started off tamely enough. Danny Fox put some Deep Heat in Gezza's boxer shorts, which obviously has an effect. Gezza being Gezza, he took that from nought to 60 immediately and approached Foxy's car, his pride and joy. Who knows what mischief he had in mind but luckily anoth player intervened before anything too drastic happened.

Next, there was a thing with people hanging other people's clothes up from the ceiling of the changing room. Again, tame enough. Then clothes were being cut up. Still fairly standard. Then someone put a dead rat in Ricko's wash bag. More rats started appearing. I got into my Mum's Focus one afternoon and there was a rat in the passenger seat with its seatbelt on.

Everyone thought Gezza was behind the invasion of the rats because he was injured and had time on his hands so somebody played another relatively harmless trick on him. Gezza retaliated. We were in the dressing room one morning, chatting and messing around, when Gezza suddenly appeared with a bag under his arm. He reached into it, hurled two snakes into the room and then slammed the door shut from the outside and held it shut.

They were totally harmless, but we didn't know that. All the lads were screaming and begging Gezza to open the door but all I could hear was him laughing his head off outside and then we realized they were fake anyway.

Take the money out of the equation and I would go back to that team and that environment in the blink of an eye. For all the bullshit and the messing about, I knew that with those players, if we went to war on the pitch, every single one of them was hardened and battle ready. I made good friends there. Sometimes the fun of football gets lost when the money rolls in. Those were happy days.

Left: The first picture of me aged 1 in fetching knitwear.

Right: Me rocking original Reeboks aged 3 or 4, sitting on the work surface. Due to some weird plumbing we always had to move the washing machine out when we wanted to use it to stop the kitchen from flooding.

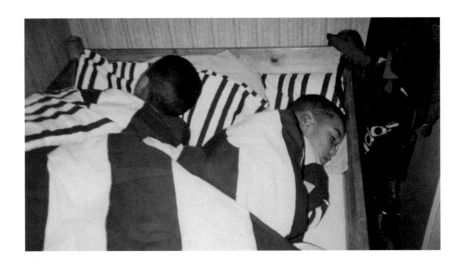

Sharing a bed with my brother, I think the morning after Christmas.
This was before the rules and regulations that prohibited sharing a bed,
but we couldn't do much else in the two-bedroom flat.

My first football kit! Christmas was big for us. My Mum saved all year and
it was the one day we were guaranteed to get spoiled. We used to do a big
Christmas shop a couple of days before and it was the one time we had things
like Pringles in the house. The rest of the year it was all own-brand products,
but Christmas was always special.

My brother and me in my Nan's back garden in 1995. That lawn always felt so vast at the time! Grandad had a pond just out of shot and he'd keep a close eye on our kickabouts in case the ball went near his beloved goldfish.

My first communion at the age of 8 or 9. A picture of innocence!

Left: My dad holding my sister at her and my brother's christening. I remember it clearly as my brother didn't like being picked up to be blessed, so he kicked my dad in the leg.

A great pic of me and my mum from when I picked up an award for playing for Chelmsley Wood's Catholic Community Centre (3Cs) Club.

The 3Cs won pretty much everything most years.
This was a treble-winning year for us.

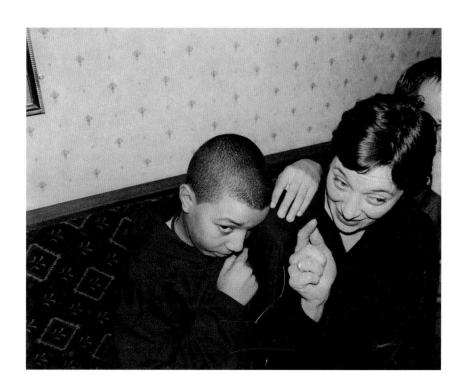

Below: Me and mum in a non-league team's bar at the age of 13. I used to do glass collecting every weekend. I would get about £40 for the weekend and the occasional fiver tip from drinkers, which I'd give to my mum. I had no use for money in those days.

Me at 20, out and about with my best mate Mark. This was quite a normal weekend scenario for me at that time.

A post-jail shot of myself and Ellis on the playstation. By the looks of it he's winning, which isn't that surprising as he quite often beat me at most things!

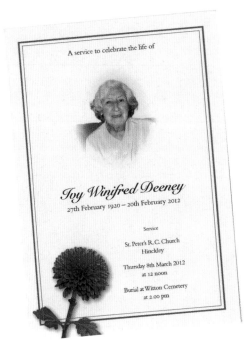

A service to celebrate the life of

Ivy Winifred Deeney

27th February 1920 – 20th February 2012

Service

St. Peter's R.C. Church
Hinckley

Thursday 8th March 2012
at 12 noon

Burial at Witton Cemetery
at 2.00 pm

Left: My Nan's order of service. I found out Dad was ill in February and she passed away not long after. She was the nicest person I'd ever met. The glue that held the family together. No problem seemed that bad when you spoke to her.

Below: My mum with Grandad. This was how you'd always find him…in a shirt with smart trousers and shoes, money in his top pocket and a pint in his hand. He was 'the man' of the family and was always there for me.

'06 10 08

CHAPTER 6

THE IMPOSTOR

I got better and better the longer I stayed at Walsall. I was playing with good players who I was able to learn from and who were generous to me with their advice, and I had good managers, too. Even Jimmy Mullen, who had a habit of calling me Ned (I think that was mainly because he couldn't remember my name was Troy), but I learned from him, too, before Chris Hutchings took over.

I had my best season at the club in 2009–10. I was the top scorer with 14 goals and I was named the Player of the Year. Other clubs were starting to take notice of me and midway through that season, I found out that Charlton Athletic had made a bid for me in the January window. That bid wasn't communicated to me at the time and Walsall rejected it.

I got a new agent that season, too. Simon Kennedy acted for Michael Ricketts and Ricko suggested I should go with him to meet Simon at the Malmaison in Birmingham. I didn't even know what the Malmaison was. It was my first time I'd been in a proper hotel. We sat down for a meal and Simon told me to get the Malburger with chips. I looked at the menu and it was £20. There was no way

I was paying that for a burger. Simon told me it was on him. He recognized a cheap date when he saw one.

Simon told me Watford were interested in signing me. He had good contacts with the club and he thought they'd be a good fit for me. We were doing well at Walsall and we ended up finishing tenth in League One in 2009–10, the club's best position in the league for six years. Watford were a mid-table Championship side and it felt like a logical next step.

Things moved quickly between me and Watford. I was aware of the money they were offering and it was life-changing for me. I'd signed a new contract at Walsall that was paying me £800 a week but Watford were offering me £6,000 a week, rising to £8,000 a week with appearance bonuses. There was also a twenty grand signing-on fee. Twenty grand hadn't been mentioned in my world, legally, ever.

I was walking around the shopping centre in Chelmsley Wood with my mates one day in that summer of 2010 when I got a call from the Watford manager Malky Mackay. We'd just come out of the bookies and we were heading to the chippy. Malky started selling the club to me but he didn't need to try too hard. I told him that with the opportunity they were offering me, I would do whatever I needed to do to make it work.

Walsall drove a hard bargain. They turned down four separate bids. They were asking for £500,000, which would have been a massive fee for a League One player at that time. There was one point where I thought the deal was done and I even passed a medical and then Walsall changed their demand and Watford threatened to pull the plug on it all.

I put in a transfer request and it all got a bit messy. The memory of what Martin Butler had said to me seemed particularly relevant around that time and I felt like I was going to have to force my way out of the club by being difficult in training. The deal was eventually agreed on the eve of the 2010–11 season. Walsall got about £350,000 in the end and a 20 per cent sell-on clause, which would have been a good deal if I hadn't stayed at Watford for the next ten years.

I was so stressed by it all, I had broken out in great big red spots. They were like heartbeats on my face. I was told that before the deal was signed, I had to go into Walsall one last time. I knew I was close to the pot of gold so I walked into Walsall and went straight to the manager's office.

I didn't know what to expect. Maybe one last plea to stay? Another twist? Chris Hutchings got up when I walked in, shook my hand and said, 'Thanks for everything, mate, you can go now.' I wasn't best pleased, to be honest, because I knew time was getting really tight to sign for Watford in time for the first game of the season. I got my boots and said goodbye to the lads and goodbye to my first club.

My Mum drove me to Beaconsfield Services on the M40 and I met an official from Watford in the car park. I sat in the car and signed my contract and she went into a local hotel, scanned it and sent it off. I was registered to play for Watford in their opening game of the season against Norwich the same day, a game that was live on television. She drove me to a meeting point on the A14 and I was dropped off there.

The Watford fitness coach picked me up and drove me to the team hotel outside Norwich. We barely said two words to each other. He didn't appear to be very happy he'd had to come and pick me up. It was the most uncomfortable drive I had ever had. I got to the hotel, was given a room key, went up, opened the door and there was a geezer getting changed in my room.

It was a lad called Dale Bennett. He looked a bit miserable. Another one who wasn't particularly pleased to see me. He said he had been selected to be on the bench for the Norwich game but now that my clearance had been through, he wasn't going to be involved any more. So they had put me in a room with the guy whose place I'd just taken.

So I made my Watford debut at Carrow Road. I came off the bench in the 58th minute to replace Marvin Sordell, who had been playing up front with Danny Graham. John Eustace and Danny had scored goals that had put us 2–1 up by that point but I was so new to everything I had to ask what Danny's name was when I came on. Malky said to call him 'DG'. It was carnage. I was whistling at people to try and get their attention so they would pass me the ball. We won the game 3–2.

I had been bought to play in attack with Danny Graham but things didn't quite work according to plan. I wasn't in the best shape, for a start. The saga of my protracted departure from Walsall had deprived me of playing time in pre-season so I wasn't match fit and I knew it would take me a little while to get up to speed.

But the main thing was that Marvin Sordell started scoring for fun. He scored five goals in four games after that Norwich match and so it was impossible for Malky to leave him out. I couldn't get in the team. We played Aldershot on a Tuesday night in the League Cup near the start of the season and I was told I would start but I was on the bench again. Danny got two, Marvin got one. I got a few minutes at the end.

And that was the pattern my season settled into. I had gone from being a big fish in a small pond to a tadpole in a lake. The idea was that I was going to be the main man but that had changed because the team was doing well without me. The more I had to wait, the worse it got. They say the devil makes work for idle hands and that was exactly what happened with me.

I was still living in Chelmsley Wood and still going out with all my mates and now I had all this money and I wasn't playing so I thought I could enjoy myself off the pitch because I wasn't being given any responsibility on the pitch. I could get drunk four or five nights a week and still be fit enough to give everything for 10 or 15 minutes at the end of a game. No problem.

I was going to clubs and buying bottles of champagne for £200. 'Only £200? Okay, we'll get ten of them.' When I was 18 or 19, everyone was paying for me. I would be drinking the WKDs, the Smirnoff alcopops, the Port and the cheap drinks. Now, I could buy my way in. Now it was my turn to pay for them. I already had the respect that came with fighting. Now I had money to spend, too.

There are a lot of wealthy footballers in Birmingham but I wasn't going to the clubs like Bamboo where they hung out because all my friends were banned from there. Mono Bar in Hurst Street was the place we went. I loved it. It was heavily Black, hip-hop, R&B, but it was closed five or six years ago because it became notorious for shootings, stabbings and brawls. I think Mono is a teppanyaki place now. I liked Sobar, too. And Dragon Eye. That's also closed now.

I was running in crazy circles. Once a month, we'd go to a different city – Cardiff, Leeds, Liverpool, Manchester – and hit the clubs there. I got glassed in the back of the head during a fight in a club in Leeds one Tuesday night and Disk drove me down to Watford training so I could be there in time on Wednesday morning. I went straight to the showers and washed the blood out my hair.

I didn't want to have to explain to Malky what had happened so I went out training as normal and decided on a plan. When we were having a practice match, I went up for a header with Tommy Aldred, who was a big defender. I engineered it so that he ran into the back of me and I went down holding my head. The physios had a look at it and saw the gash and I got it stitched up with no one any the wiser.

Mostly, I still went out in Birmingham. There was a club called Rococo on Broad Street on a Tuesday night. Sunday and Tuesday were the best nights. Tuesday, you could get in there early and watch the Champions League football and get shots for £1, like it was a student night. I'd get out of Rococo at 3.30am, get a taxi from Broad Street to the train station, get the first train from New Street to Watford at 4.30am, have a sleep in the car at the training ground and then train. Then I'd get the train home and sleep. That was a normal week. If we got an extra day off on Monday, I'd be out Saturday, Sunday, Monday, Tuesday.

Did it all go to my head? Oh yeah. I was the man back home all of a sudden. I just turned into a tornado. You've got a kid who's had absolutely nothing for his whole life. I had a couple of pairs of trainers to my name and that's about it. Then you give that kid thousands of pounds a week and tell him he can do all the things he ever wanted to do.

You can give your Mum money, you can go out with the boys when you want, you can be one of the lads. I was liked but I wasn't really one of the lads until I started earning proper money because I couldn't afford to keep up. I was just Little Troy. All my mates had cars, houses, gold chains, watches. I had fuck all. Then it's 'Here you go, Troy, you can do everything you want to do in ten seconds' and I had no guidance. I just spent it.

My first pay cheque at Watford, I cleared £16,000. I'm the man then. Let's have a tear-up. I was buying more trainers and track suits than I knew what to do with. My core friends were all there. We were all on the journey. We all got flung into it. We all got flung into this tornado of me being noticed and valued. So we'd go into Sobar and now the Villa lads wanted to speak to me.

It was strange for all of us. I was 22 and on an incredible journey. No one told me to invest or that I was actually earning peanuts compared to what the top players were earning. Because in my mind, I was a millionaire. And also, I didn't believe it was going to last. I thought it would only last for a short time so I might as well have a good bash at it before I was returned to obscurity and being a nobody.

I had impostor syndrome. Yeah, 100 per cent I did. That is my life from the age of nine to twenty-five. That's it. Impostor syndrome. The fear of not being good enough. Someone will find out that you're not that guy or you're not as good as you make yourself out to be on the surface. That was how I thought about my personal life as well as my playing career. When you boil it all down, it was all fear.

The best way to describe how I was acting is to compare it to that guy who won £10m on the lottery, spent all his money and had a demolition derby in his back garden, smashing cars up. When people aren't ready or conditioned to have fame and money and you throw somebody in there, it does weird and wonderful things to you. That's what it did to me.

From the age of 17, I was playing men's football with 35 year olds and happy to hold my own physically and in terms of banter. I have always been outgoing and loud and I love to make people laugh. I like to be the funny person. Now you throw thousands of pounds in the mix and a little bit of fame, and what a cocktail that was. Right, we're all going out, we're all having a laugh, I'll foot the bill on most occasions and we'll have a tear-up.

When people told me to calm down, I'd say: 'Why? Fuck that. It's going to be over soon. I've only got two or three years of this.' The football wasn't saving me either. Because Marvin Sordell and Danny Graham were doing so well, I could afford to go out and get pissed.

And so we drank, we had a good time, and if we had a scrap, it was an even better night. It was fun to have a scrap. We didn't go out to start a fight but we never backed down from one. What did I like about it? The adrenaline of it. In the venues we were in, there would be two to three fights per night, clear up the glass and carry on.

Me and all of my group might be what others would call wrong'uns but our hearts and intentions were pure and as we have grown up and seen more of the world, that side of us has died down. It is an easy cop-out but you are a product of your environment. The environment didn't give a shit if you were a solid worker that worked nine to five. Instead it was 'How much money have you got, what chains can you get, what drinks are you drinking?' and all that egotistical bullshit.

You only know what you know and as long as people respected us around the area and we had a nice motor and birds wanted us and juvenile shit like that, that was all that mattered. We didn't really care. I was on a crazy ride. My first year at Watford was an absolute write-off, up and down the country, different nightclubs, different scraps.

I had bought my first house in Chelmsley for £126,000 on a right-to-buy deal. I had a white Mercedes. My bills were about a grand and I was probably spending about three grand a weekend. There's a party on Tuesday, I'll be there. There's a party on Thursday, I'll be there. At the end of that first season, Danny Graham had 27 goals, Marvin Sordell had 15 and I had three.

Malky Mackay was great, by the way. He spent a lot of time trying to mould me into a footballer. One day, he took me across the road from the training ground to Costa and asked me what was going on. I had a lot of issues, obviously. We sat and chatted for an hour. He was brilliant. He did everything he could to get the best out of me.

I didn't really know how to talk to him or express this stuff. He used to say he wanted to get me down to Watford more so he could keep an eye on me. I don't blame him for that. I was using living in Birmingham as an excuse a lot of the time. I'd not turn up to training and I'd blame the traffic. Except, I forgot John Eustace and Martin Taylor lived in Birmingham, too, and they didn't seem to encounter traffic on their journeys. I was making it fairly obvious I was lying.

Watford must have despaired of me but they didn't really have the budget for anyone else. I was the budget. All the money had gone on me. I didn't know that. I thought it would be like Walsall. I was drinking and playing when I was there but when you are drinking and playing and scoring, no one gives a toss. They let you get away with things. But now I was drinking and not playing and not scoring so if you didn't turn up on a Monday, people wanted to know what the hell was going on.

The whole narrative had changed. Nobody was making excuses for me any more. I couldn't blame them. If you watch *The Last Dance*, the documentary series about Michael Jordan and the Chicago Bulls, everyone knew how good Dennis Rodman was and so they turned the other way when he went to have a few days in Las Vegas. They were happy to say, 'Go and have a few days and come back when you're ready.' In sport, we will always make allowances for people when they are performing.

Malky was unbelievably good with me. I know that he was criticized for some of the things he said and did at Cardiff later in his managerial career but I can't speak about that because I wasn't there. I just know what he was like with me. He must have thought I was a waste of time. He was probably thinking, *Why am I putting my neck on the line for this prick?* I would have. But he never, ever showed that kind of anger.

When Malky left to take over at Cardiff in the summer of 2011, his assistant, Sean Dyche, took over. Dychey had been really good with me up until that point. He was straight. He said he rated me but he also said that unless I improved my attitude, I wouldn't make it.

I didn't want to listen. I would see on-loan Jordon Mutch come on and I would feel resentful that he had gone straight into the team and I hadn't. I'd tell myself they didn't rate me and I'd use that as a justification for why I didn't need to try. When Dychey took over as manager, I was told at the start of that pre-season that he didn't see a future for me at the club. He thought I was a pisshead and that I didn't listen and that he was going to try to break me in pre-season training.

But I refused to be broken. It was hard physical work. We went somewhere in France for a ten-day boot camp. We did bleep tests. Dychey made me train with the midfielders, not the strikers, because they worked harder and they would show me up more.

Every time we did a run or a drill, Dychey would be shouting out, 'Come on, Troy, are you going to quit yet, do you need a day off?'

They had lost respect for me at that point. I wasn't reliable. They didn't trust me. In hindsight, I don't blame them. Another day, they took us on the beach. It was tipping down and he had us running races up and down these long flights of steps from the beach up to the promenade. We'd keep going until Dychey decided we were knackered and then we would start jogging on the sand again.

Then they had an outside circuit set up and we had five rounds of that. Adrian Mariappa, who had become a good friend, was urging me not to let them break me, but it was getting to me. Dychey made us face the water and then he said 'run' and we had to run straight into the water and then that was it. It was over.

On the last night in France, he said we could go out and have a bite to eat and a few beers. 'But don't let Troy drink,' he said. And I didn't have a drink because I thought, *If I have a drink, he's won.* The next morning, Dychey was asking what I got up to the night before and he didn't believe it when the other lads told him that I hadn't touched a drop.

I didn't get much a sniff in the first half of the 2011–12 season and I knew Watford were trying to move me on to Coventry City and replace me with Lee Novak, who was at Huddersfield Town. The deal broke down for some reason and I stayed. And then on the last day of the January 2012 transfer window, we were preparing for a game away at Millwall when we were told the club had sold Marvin Sordell to Bolton Wanderers.

My attitude had been gradually improving after that summer camp in France and so once Marvin had gone, Dychey stuck me into the side alongside Joe Garner in attack for the Millwall match. It was all very last-minute but I understood this could be a second chance. Dychey had started to trust me more and I was keen to repay him for that. I scored ten minutes before half time, Joe scored in the second half and we won 2-0.

I scored again ten days later against Nottingham Forest at the City Ground and went on a scoring run. Things were turning around for me on the pitch. My attitude was better and I loved the fact that I had proved Dychey wrong. I realized that all he wanted was reliability and I was getting to a point where I could provide that.

He has a reputation as an uncompromising character but he is not all horrible. I found him a very funny individual. He is personable, he has got a good mix of the way he handles players and the media and even now, after everything he has achieved at Burnley on a really low budget, he is still underrated. What he has done at that club is unreal and I have a great deal of respect for him and for his assistant Ian Woan.

So I thought I was on the way back. I thought I was about to fulfil all the potential people had seen in me when I moved to Watford in the first place. But then two things happened: my Dad rang and asked me to go with him to a hospital appointment, something he had never done before. The second thing? I went on a night out that changed my life.

CHAPTER 7

THE STRONGEST MAN
I KNEW

It was a Sunday in late February 2012 when Dad called. I was having a lie-in and I woke up to three missed calls from him. I knew something must be wrong. If he called once, he'd usually just leave a message or ask me to call him back. If he called me twice, I knew it was important. I wondered if he might be in some sort of trouble with the police.

I called him back. I asked him if he was okay. 'Sound,' he said. But he said he had a doctor's appointment at the Queen Elizabeth Hospital in Birmingham the next day and he'd like me to drive him there. He told me after the appointment he had been trying to ignore pain in his chest and throat for six months. He was old-school. He didn't like hospitals, didn't like pills, didn't like doctors. It was only when he started getting short of breath while he was walking that he decided he had to do something about it.

I think he had probably left it for a long time before he'd gone to get himself checked over. Too long. He hated going to the doctor. I think he probably saw it as a sign of weakness. Going to the doctor was a bit too much like asking for help and Dad didn't like doing that in any aspect of his life. Even getting me to drive him round there was unusual. I had an uneasy feeling about it all.

Me and my ex-partner drove round on Monday morning and picked him and his partner up. He was trying to deflect and make me laugh and do different stuff, anything to move the subject away from the fact we were going to the doctor's. We got there and we were waiting and I still didn't know why we were there. He hadn't shared any information with us. He was hoping it was all nothing.

They called us in and as we were walking into the consulting room, Dad took me to one side and said he had had a scan on a lump in his chest and the doctor had called him back to talk about the results of it. I had a thousand questions. My Granddad had had cancer and then died from a heart attack. So I knew about cancer. My ex-partner's Nan had passed away with it as well.

We sat down and the doctor started talking. My Dad had this thing about looking a man in the eye when you are talking. He was obsessed with it. Like a lot of things with him, he said it was about respect. At least show a man the respect of looking him in the eye when you are talking to him. This doctor was talking to us but he had his head down and his eyes fixed on the table in front of him.

The doctor started telling him the results of the scan. He said it was a problem in his throat. His oesophagus. He said it was cancer and it was at an advanced stage and they would need to start treatment on Friday. He said that my Dad would need chemotherapy to have any chance of curing it. He still wouldn't look him in the eye. So my Dad smacked his hand down on the paper where the guy was writing and said: 'Could you look at me when you are telling me what's going on?'

It was the first time I had ever heard worry in his voice. He wasn't dominant like he normally was. He was almost pleading. I started asking all the questions. I knew what to ask because I had been through this before with others. That seemed to settle my Dad down a bit because he didn't know anything about cancer.

I think he was probably in shock because he had been hoping it wouldn't be bad news. I guess that's the way most of us approach things like that. Just hope it's never going to happen. I asked what the treatment was and the doctor said it would be chemo. I asked if there was anything dietary we could do and he just said chemo again. My Dad looked at him and said: 'Thanks for fuck all.' He said he'd decide about whether he wanted to have chemotherapy or not. He was trying to wrestle back control.

It was really difficult for all of us. I had never seen my Dad vulnerable before. I'd seen him collared by the police but I'd never seen him emotionally vulnerable. He had always been in a position of power but now someone else – or something else – had the power and it was hard for us to deal with the reality of that. It was shocking.

We walked out of the consulting room and Dad's partner started crying. 'Don't fucking cry,' he said. 'Don't embarrass me.' So we had the quietest, slowest walk to the car you can ever imagine. I asked if he wanted me to take him home and he told me to take him to the pub. He said if he wasn't in the pub by 2pm, people would know something was wrong.

I drove him into the centre of town and there was a pub underneath the ramp to the Oasis that was a real dive. I was upset as well but he wasn't crying so I wasn't allowed to cry either. I could see all the thoughts going through his head but this was old-school: we don't talk and we don't cry. So I dropped him off and he said he'd call me tomorrow. 'I'll have a beer and then I'll be all right,' he said.

Most of all, he was just really angry with the doctor because the doctor wouldn't look at him. He said he felt he had been in with a used-car salesman. He couldn't understand how this man was dealing with somebody's life and he couldn't look at him. That was the thing that wound him up more than being told he had cancer. Or maybe that was just the only way he knew of dealing with the anxiety. Perhaps it was easier to personalize it.

I look back now and think I should have done more to help. I have a lot of regrets. I wasn't on the kind of money I was earning when I was playing in the Premier League but my first deal with Watford meant I was well paid. I certainly had enough money to get him a specialist and private health care, but I didn't know any better then. I hadn't actually used private healthcare myself.

I think maybe the cancer was too advanced anyway but I don't know that for sure. Maybe someone else could have got him to do chemo if we had gone down the private healthcare route. As it was, he refused to have chemotherapy because of the way the doctor had spoken to him. That was what he said, anyway. Maybe it was just another way of not really confronting it. We tried some holistic approaches. They didn't work.

I found it hard to deal with. So I tried to forget about it. I was given my Dad's diagnosis on the Monday and later in the week, it was also the anniversary of my Great-Nan passing away. And then there was the fact that it was Disk's birthday. So that was a great excuse to go out and get wasted. In a lot of people's lives, you associate good times with drink. So it was his birthday and we were going out and we were going to have a good time for his birthday.

What I didn't realize then but what I know now is associating drink with a good time is cool but drinking when you are anxious, sad and angry exacerbates all those feelings and fuels them. That night we went out was the night after I had found out about my Dad's condition and the rush of emotions pushed me right up to that limit and then took me over the edge.

We drove up from Chelmsley Wood together. There were a few cars full of the lads and probably about 12 of us in total. My brother Ellis was out, too, with some of his friends. We parked the cars on a side road somewhere close to Broad Street, hit a couple of bars and then headed over to Rococo, where we spent the rest of the night.

We left the club about 3am, obviously drunk. I was on the phone. I was in that drunken blaze of head-down walking, not really aware of anything around me, just me in my own addled world, anaesthetized by drink but simmering under the surface, ready to blow if something goes wrong or somebody says the wrong thing.

I wasn't really thinking about anything. There had been no issues in the club. There hadn't been any fights. We'd all had a good time. I was vaguely aware of some shouting going on but it was at the periphery of my consciousness. Broad Street is a long road of bars and clubs, and at kicking-out time there is always someone being raucous or wanting to fight. Most of the time, it's just noise.

I didn't know this at the time because I was a little way up ahead but when some of the lads who were with me walked past the entrance to a club called Bliss, there was a bit of a kerfuffle going on. It was bad timing, really. There was trouble inside Bliss and the bouncer on the door knew that a load of people were about to be kicked out so he wanted to clear the area around the exit.

The bouncer pushed a couple of my mates and they took exception. There was an argument, then the lads who were causing trouble in Bliss got kicked out and started fighting with my mates. Then another group of people came over and got involved and all of a sudden there was a brawl going on. I was unaware of all this. But then someone came up to me and said something about my brother. They said he was in a fight.

I turned round and in the blurriness, I just saw arms and fists going everywhere. I thought, *What the hell's going on there?* I started walking towards it and it was getting more and more clear but there were more and more people. There were three different groups of people fighting. The closer I got, the more chaotic everything got and the more agitated I felt. Before you know it, everyone is heated, everyone is drunk and it's intertwined.

All I thought was *My brother's in there somewhere* and I just lost my head. I just ran into the middle of it. I was looking for Ellis and hitting anything that moved that was in the way. I was like someone clearing out a ruck in a rugby match.

In a split second, I had forgotten who I was and what I was. I just went in and steam-rollered anything and anyone who was in the way. I could just see a commotion and I thought, *Right, until I find my brother, someone's in the way.* The only people I didn't hit were people I knew. Everyone else was a target.

I hit one lad and he fell against the side of a taxi that was in the rank on Broad Street. The taxis all moved along because the drivers were worried their vehicles were going to get damaged. This lad – he was a student – went down but as I turned around to start fighting again, I felt him tugging at my leg.

If you know fighting, if someone's grabbing at you, there's a chance he's got a weapon. You don't know what he's got. So I kicked him in the head. I just put him out. That's the only part I don't like talking about. That could have gone so far left. The guy could have died because I am a powerful guy. I didn't think about my actions. When the police showed me the video the next day, I couldn't watch.

It was as if I was meant to be caught. You can't really see me at the start of the CCTV footage because all the taxis are in the way. But then, after I've hit this guy and he's fallen into the side of the taxi, all the taxis move along and it is like the waves parting and suddenly I'm standing there, right in the middle of the footage just as I kick the lad in the head.

I was right in line with the camera. I kicked him and carried on scrapping. I never once checked to see if he was all right. All I felt was someone pulling on my leg and I thought he was going to stab me. I turned and kicked him and put him out so I didn't have to worry about him any more. It's brutal. The kid was defenceless and I kicked him in the head, with all the power I possess. Then we ran up the road.

I knew the police were coming. I could hear sirens. I knew how it worked. I knew I had to get off the main drag. I turned left and I thought I had got away. Then I realized my brother wasn't with me. It was his first time out of town and he didn't know where he was going. I turned round and saw him running straight down Broad Street, exactly the place you are going to get caught.

Until that moment, I thought I'd try and get away. I knew I'd done something wrong but flight is still a powerful human instinct. I knew where the cars were parked so I was going to go back there and lie down in the back seat and throw something over myself to conceal my presence. But when I saw Ellis running up Broad Street, I knew I had to turn around and get him. I couldn't go home without him. My Mum would have never forgiven me.

So I caught up with him, grabbed him and threw him back the way we were supposed to go. We'd only gone a few yards when the police arrived and jumped on us. We were thrown into the back of a police van and taken to a small jail at the back of Broad Street, the Steelhouse Lane Lock-up, which was where the mugshots of the notorious Peaky Blinders were taken in the old days.

It was an old Victorian holding cell, a staging post for idiots like me between arrest and the courts. People told them I was a footballer and asked them to leave me alone but that wasn't particularly helpful. Funnily enough, there's not too much sympathy around for anyone who's behaved as I had just behaved. Saying I'm a footballer is just going to make matters worse.

I spent the night in a cell in Steelhouse Lane. It wasn't one of my better nights of sleep. I was starving, hungover and cold as ice and I was in pain from the working over I'd got. I didn't feel sorry for myself. I knew what I'd done. I knew I deserved to be in there.

I imagine there's an assumption that I was worried about my football career. I probably should have been, but I never once thought about football. I was in a strange place in my life at that point. I was good at putting stuff away in compartments and forgetting about them, or at least pushing them to the back of my consciousness.

And, anyway, this was my world. I wasn't exactly a stranger to stuff like this. I didn't make a habit of kicking people in the head but I wasn't some wide-eyed innocent who was suddenly in a blind panic. Fighting is a chaotic thing and at that moment I didn't really have a clear recollection of everyone I had hit or kicked. That would come later when I saw the video footage.

The first person I called was my Dad, the person who had been in jail more often than anyone else I knew. I told him what had happened, that there had been a brawl, that I'd kicked somebody, that I'd run and that we'd been caught. I asked him what was going to happen to me. He was unconcerned. He said, 'Oh, you'll be all right.' He made it sound like it was an inconvenience. Something rather trifling.

The morning after, they came to get me out of the cell and took me to an interrogation room. It reminded me of a scene from *The Bill*. I started chatting to the geezer, who showed me the video of what had happened the night before. It made me wince. He said the student I'd kicked was in hospital. When they showed me the video, I felt sick. I was charged with affray and they asked me what I wanted to do. I said I'd plead guilty. There was not a thought in my mind of contesting it. I knew what I'd done.

I was sorry for what I'd done. I said the kid had nothing to do with it. I had a son of my own and I knew that if I was being shown the video and it was my son, I would be angry. They said I'd go home and I would be sent a court date.

I phoned my Dad and told him the charge was affray. He said: 'Don't worry about that, it's a load of bollocks, you'll be sweet, first-time offender, it'll be community service at worst, don't worry about it, go home, rest up, I'll come and see you later.'

So as far as I was concerned, that was it. I've said I'm guilty, my Dad's told me it'll be nothing, so I can just go and get on with my life until my court appearance, which was scheduled for six weeks later. Simon, my agent, sorted out a legal team, my Mum told me I was an idiot and I tried to ice my ankle because I knew I had to go and tell Dychey what had happened.

We had Wednesday off so I went into training on Thursday and told Dychey what had happened. 'Fucking hell, Troy,' he said,

'I thought we had got over this kind of thing. I thought we had broken the back of the nonsense. I thought we had got through to you. You've been behaving, you've been on time. And now this happens.'

I managed to train despite the pain in my ankle. News of my arrest broke late that week and it made a few of the papers. We played Burnley at Vicarage Road on the Saturday after my arrest and I scored the winner in a 3–2 victory. Watford fans were singing songs about 'Deeney hates the police' and I genuinely found it funny. I know that looks appalling and I wonder what the hell I was doing. That's where I was. I knew the legal team was taking care of it. In my thought process, it was all gone.

It is strange how crises affect different people in sport in different ways. I remember that when Jonathan Woodgate and Lee Bowyer faced charges relating to an attack on an Asian student, Sarfraz Najeib, in Leeds city centre in 2000, Woodgate looked thin and gaunt and his performances suffered. Bowyer played some of the best football of his career.

Similarly, the fact that I was facing a charge of affray didn't affect my football at all. I had started playing well just before the incident in Broad Street and I continued to play well after it. In fact, I went on a scoring spree. I scored against Burnley and then I scored six more in the last eleven league games of the season, including the last four games in succession.

At the end of the season, I went to Las Vegas with about 15 of the Watford lads. I had a great time with them. We stayed at the MGM

Grand and went to the Floyd Mayweather v Miguel Cotto fight, which was in the Grand Garden Arena at the hotel complex. I had been saving up for that trip since December. I wasn't going to let an impending court case get in the way of enjoying it.

I was only in Vegas for five days but when I got back, I had a message to say I had to go and see my Dad straight away. I was told he was fading fast. A few weeks before I flew to the States, he had started spitting blood so he had finally agreed to go into hospital. He was in the Queen Elizabeth for a couple of weeks but the cancer was attacking him aggressively.

Even then, I never thought my Dad was going to die. He was the strongest bloke I knew. He was feeling worse and worse, but he was still walking and was still able to get around. I went to Vegas for five days and I came back, landed at Heathrow, got the train back to Birmingham International and the second I got there, people said, 'We've got to go and see your Dad.'

He was in QE and he was in a wheelchair. I had been gone five days. What the hell had happened? They said that because he had refused treatment, the cancer had spread even more rapidly. In my mind, he was still this big Thor-like character, this gladiator, and he went from that to a frail old man in weeks. He was 47 years old. From being so independent to being dependent like that, I think that destroyed him. He made the decision that he wasn't going to die in hospital so he went to his mate Micky's house for a few days.

They had a barbecue in the back garden so everybody could come and see him. My Dad would normally be the life and soul of that kind of thing. This time, he wasn't. At one point, he even went off for a nap. He went back into hospital for a while but then he came out one last time and he went to stay with his sister, my Auntie Sarah. He was a smoker, a drinker and a fighter and she was a God-fearing woman.

That was where he wanted to be. He had been told he was going to die and he wanted to be in a place of peace. She looked after him and bathed him and all those different things. She read the Bible to him at night and made up a bed for him in her living room so that nurses could come round and care for him. His mum had come back from Jamaica to help look after him.

My Dad had vowed he'd see my son's third birthday and Myles was three on 30 May. My family went out for a pub dinner with Myles on that day, sat down to eat and ordered a drink and at that moment, I got a text from a relative saying, 'Your Dad's going, you need to come back to the house.' We had to leave Myles having his birthday dinner with his Nan.

I went to spend the last few hours with Dad. He made it through the night. I remember his breaths were laboured because he had cancer of the oesophagus. It was like his breath was trying to get round a golf ball that was lodged in his throat. So every breath was like three different breaths. It was horrible. That's your king, lying there.

Despite everything that had happened, despite the bad things, despite all the bullshit, there was so much love between us. He was the guy who taught me how to play football and looked after me. My sense of humour comes from him. Loads of things about me come from him and we were getting to a good place. I felt like we were becoming better and better friends.

There was so much unfinished business. The man never went on holiday. For all the stories I've told you, the man had a heart of gold. He would do anything for his kids. I was haunted by a few things. I still am. What if I had sorted myself out earlier and got into football earlier and took things seriously, would we have had better healthcare from a younger age? Would he have slowed down?

I had only had three years as a professional footballer. I had only just begun to understand what this football stuff could do. I had only just begun to understand the power it could wield and the doors it could open. Maybe I could have done more for him. Even now, when I get on a flight to go on holiday, there is always a little bit in the back of my mind that my Dad never got to do this.

It's not a negative, really. It's more that I'm determined to live my life because life's short. He died at 47 and while he lived a somewhat chaotic life, he never really lived. He never really grew up. He was an adult, but he still had that little bit of immaturity left in him. He had that weird 'I'm still young' vibe about him. That adult that we all know who still tries to dress a little bit young.

With him, it wasn't that he tried to dress young but he had that mentality that he still felt he was in his thirties and because he was in good nick, maybe he didn't feel like he had aged properly. When you have spent time in jail, when you have missed your own birthdays and other people's birthdays and you have missed landmarks in life, time stops. I have got friends who have done a few years in jail and say they go in at 22 and come out at 25, but they are still mentally 22. In jail, everything stops.

My superhero had just gone in less than three months and it concentrated my mind. At the time of writing this I'm 33. It's only 14 years from now if that's all I've got left. It makes me want to make sure I get my affairs in order. He didn't leave anybody with anything apart from the fact he had an unbelievable street credibility. If I was to die at any point soon, there is money for the kids and properties for the family and that was a lesson I took from it.

As I mentioned, they had turned the front room at Auntie Sarah's into a bedroom for my Dad. This big personality was there, gasping for breath and drinking through a straw. All things he would have seen as demeaning and weak had all now been visited upon him. I wanted to take some of the pain and make it peaceful for him, but it wasn't like that, unfortunately.

The whole family was there. All my cousins and my Dad's brothers and sisters. That whole morning was slightly joyous because everyone was together. When we were in the room with dad it was terrible but the second you stepped out, you saw cousins you hadn't seen for years and everyone was telling old stories about Dad.

I said my goodbyes to him and I stepped outside for a while. My Granddad was flying in from Jamaica and everyone was hoping he would arrive in time to see his son. They had flown into Heathrow, but they had got stuck in traffic on the M25 and I heard someone say that someone who was in the car with my Granddad had phoned to say they were a few minutes away.

We were all looking forward to seeing Granddad and then I heard one of the older ladies inside just scream. I knew. I knew dad had died. We went in and one of my Nan's friends took her scarf off and held his head and wrapped it round his jaw so that his mouth wouldn't be open and my sister was screaming at her to get off him. Then we looked up and my granddad had just pulled up. I thought it was as if my dad had known his dad had arrived and that he would look after everything and so it was okay for him to let go. The fight was over.

I will never forget it. My Granddad had worked at Royal Mail for a long time and he was always a happy presence in my life when I was younger. When he retired, he went back to Jamaica and I don't think he had any intention of returning to England but my Dad's illness changed that. He walked in and saw my Dad lying there and he just burst into tears.

If you had asked me ten ways my Dad would have died, I wouldn't have named cancer. He was the strongest man I knew. If cancer could take him, it could take anyone.

I walked to the corner with my brother and we were in floods of tears. There were kids playing football further down the road and this lad came up to me and said, 'I'm so sorry.' It was a truly surreal moment. I felt like a part of me had died as well. I had to figure it all out on my own now.

Three of the five people that raised me had died in a short space of time. I was also due to go to court in a couple of weeks and I knew by then that I was going to go to jail. I wanted to look out for my brother and sister. I felt even more responsibility for them now that Dad was gone. It was one of my saddest days. I'm not quite over it. I don't think I ever will be.

CHAPTER 8

THE LONG PATH TO REDEMPTION

We buried my Dad on a Friday. The following Monday, I went to jail. It is not what you usually envisage when you think of a long weekend. But they were two seminal events in my life, two moments that have shaped the years that have passed since and, in their different ways, set me on the long path to the redemption that I am still trying to achieve.

I understood my Dad more in the days following his death than I ever really had in life. I was asked to do the eulogy at his funeral and so I spoke to a lot of his old friends to do my research. I wanted to do a proper job. I wanted to do him justice and give him the farewell he deserved, so I sought out all the old stories about him.

I guess a lot of his friends were criminals. It feels stark when you stick that label on someone and I knew a lot of them as more layered characters than that. There are criminals who never go to jail and there are good men who spend parts of their lives behind bars and do more for those around them than many people in our society ever do.

Life is not black and white like that. My Dad did some bad things. There were times when he bullied my Mum and there were times when he frightened me and there were times – many times – when he found himself on the wrong side of the law. But what was the main thing he did in his life? He looked after someone else's son when he didn't have to. He looked after his other kids, too.

However dysfunctional it may seem to other people in a different level of society, he gave us a framework and an idea of right and wrong. Even if he did not always practise what he preached, that idea lodged with us somewhere and after many years of groping my way towards it, I have got closer to standing by the principles he said I should adhere to.

That is also part of the reason why I still bristle if someone hears parts of my childhood story and assumes I must have been desperately unhappy. Because I wasn't. I know it probably sounds absurd to someone from a middle-class background, say, who judges happiness by a different frame of reference, but I'll say it again: I consider that I had a happy childhood.

It had its bad moments and it was as complicated as hell in terms of my identity and a deep-seated confusion about my Dad and my biological father. And I'm still having therapy to try to deal with that and to fix some of the shortcomings that were sown in me. But at the same time, I'm also thankful for what I was given and I'm thankful for my Mum and Dad.

And yeah, maybe my childhood led me inexorably to jail. I think that if I had got away with what I did that night on Broad Street, it would only have been a matter of time until I did something else that would have put me in jail. If I had not been punished for it, it would only have increased the idea that had grown in me that I was untouchable. That I was invincible.

If I had got away with it, I would have done it again. Somehow, somewhere. I would have punched somebody else or kicked somebody else. The only difference is that it would have taken longer. I would have been another year older. Another year closer to the grave. And that would have meant there would have been one less year for me to put things right and to make the change in my life I needed to make.

And if my childhood led me inexorably to jail, then it also led me out of jail and into a new life. It made me want to fix things. It made me want to live the kind of life that my Dad was finally starting to live when he was diagnosed with cancer. It was too late for him by the time he started to change and I didn't want it to be too late for me.

His mates all said the same thing to me when I was preparing his eulogy. 'Your Dad was a stand-up guy.' That was the common theme. Every story they told me was funny to them in a crazy, criminal way. 'We were getting chased by the police and your Dad pulled this amazing handbrake turn and we were back facing the other way before the police even realized.'

I was listening to these stories and thinking, *I'm not sure I can regale the mourners at his funeral with a story about a car chase.* They all talked, too, about how he would be there for them if they needed him. They talked about what a loyal friend he was. They talked about how he was as hard as nails. And about how, when he had had a drink, he could start an argument in an empty house.

At the funeral, my Dad's body lay in an open casket. I liked the open casket. In my experience, it is seen in the Black community as the honourable thing to have your casket open so that people can come and pay their final respects and perhaps gain a sense of closure.

The most famous example is probably Emmett Till's funeral in 1955, one of the events that sparked the civil-rights movement in the US. There was an added motive for an open casket in that instance, of course. Till had been brutally murdered by two white men and his mother wanted the world to see what they had done. That story was something that made a huge impression on me.

I was lucky I was able to be there at my Dad's funeral. My court appearance had originally been scheduled for the end of May, but thankfully the legal team that was acting for me got it pushed it back a couple of weeks. If my court date hadn't been changed, it would have been difficult for me to get out of prison so soon after the start of my sentence. Even in the best-case scenario, I'd have had to turn up in handcuffs and with guards. It wouldn't have been quite the spectacle anyone had intended.

In the end, my Dad's funeral was moving in a different way. He had a young son by then, my youngest brother, Caiden, who would have been four or five when Dad died. Dad took him everywhere with him. He absolutely doted on him. He was becoming the Dad that we had all wanted when we were younger, the Dad that he wasn't quite ready to become back then. He did everything with Caiden. They were inseparable.

As the priest came out to begin the service, Caiden got up of his own accord and went over to the casket and put his hand on my Dad's hand and the whole place started sobbing. There were more than 200 people at that funeral and I think every one of them was crying. He didn't move for an hour, that kid. People who never cried were crying that day.

Everyone who went up to do a speech couldn't finish it so I ended up doing about four speeches plus my own. Then we carried him out in the coffin. When we got to the cemetery, we lowered him into the grave and let some doves go. As soon as we put him in the grave, it started pouring down. The rain fell and fell and fell and everyone was drenched.

It is also our tradition to fill in the grave ourselves once the casket has been lowered into it and as the rain fell, the clay started to get really thick and heavy. We were all wearing suits and some of the men who had come to take part in this element of the ceremony hung back because they didn't want to ruin their clothes or get expensive shoes dirty.

Some of the Zulus were there, my Dad's old football crew, and one of them, who was busy shovelling the dirt into the grave, turned round to the rest and shouted at them for worrying more about their shoes than taking part in what had to be done. More people joined in then and we worked away in the rain until the job was done.

We had the wake at the Irish Centre in Solihull. It had been a long day and a lot of the people there were emotionally drained. It was made more difficult for me by the fact that Colin Hemmings, my biological father, was the DJ that night. That unsettled me. I found it very weird, that collision of the two men who were my father.

Only one of them was my Dad, but that part of it was strange, too. My Dad was dead and Colin Hemmings was playing him out. My Dad was dead and Colin Hemmings was playing records at the funeral. My Dad was dead but I knew that he would always be with me. Colin Hemmings was alive, but he meant nothing to me. He was present, but he was the man who wasn't there. The man who had never been there.

He came over to me at one point. He said he was sorry about my Dad and asked if I wanted to have a chat. Having a chat with him was just about the last thing I wanted to do, especially at that moment. I told him it wasn't the right time. It'll never be the right time. He went back to his turntable and the music started again.

There was another kind of problem towards the end of the evening. I guess altercations are not that uncommon at funerals, when people are emotional and they are getting drunk to try to blot out some of the pain they are feeling. That's what I've used drink for a lot in my life. I understand why people do it. So it wasn't really a surprise that there was a fight at my Dad's funeral. Most of his life had been accompanied by fighting. So why not his death, too?

A lot of the people there weren't exactly shrinking violets. There were men there with a lot of connections, men who had big reputations in a certain section of Birmingham society. There were people who were loyal old friends of my Dad, but there were also a few people with grudges. There was a lot of love but there was also a lot of tension.

I was talking with some friends late in the evening when I looked over to another part of the bar and saw my sister, who was about 14 then, talking to a couple of geezers who had just walked in. I watched them for a minute and saw her burst into tears and run out of the room.

It turned out they were people who hadn't been invited and one of them had said something inappropriate to my sister about my Dad, something uncomplimentary. This geezer was all mouth now my Dad wasn't there. He was a nobody who would never have dared say anything like that when my Dad was alive.

I didn't do anything immediately. A few minutes later, someone came up to me and told me to follow him and not ask any questions. We found the geezer who had upset my sister at the bar carrying on as if nothing had happened and we confronted him. We threw him outside and the people at the Irish Centre suggested fairly firmly that we should call it a night.

That weekend was just like any other weekend. I knew by then that my sentencing hearing on Monday would end with me going to jail, but I didn't want to acknowledge that with my family. So we didn't do anything special. I didn't go on an outing with my son Myles or anything like that. We didn't talk about what was going to happen. That was how it was back then. That was how I was. I didn't talk about anything.

I'd found out I would be sent down when I was at Chester Races the previous month. My lawyer was there and he was adamant that I would get a jail sentence. Everything I'd been told about it being my first offence and only a charge of affray and the fact that that would save me was wrong, he said. I was surprised because of what my Dad had said to the contrary but it didn't bother me particularly.

I went out on to the balcony in the private box that Simon, my agent, had arranged for me at the racecourse, watched the races and had a beer. I went back into Troy mode. 'Everyone's here. Let's fuck it off and have a beer.' I thought I might as well enjoy it. I wasn't thinking about the repercussions, how I was going to get by, how my family would survive, what would happen to my career.

I had a matter-of-fact approach to everything then. If that was what was going to happen, I thought, then I might as well just get on with it. I didn't say goodbye to Myles, when I left home that morning. I went about it like a normal day. Myles went to school. I didn't bring anything with me that I could take to jail, no clothes, no photos, no mementoes. It was as if it wasn't happening. I was acting pretty cool but actually I was just numb.

And so, on the morning of Monday 25 June 2012, I walked through the main entrance of Birmingham Crown Court to hear my sentence for what I had done a few months earlier. I recognized the Lock-up on Steelhouse Lane, where I had been taken in the aftermath of the brawl, as I was on my way in. It was just round the corner from the Crown Court.

Four of us were sentenced that day. Ellis was sentenced to eight months in prison, suspended for 18 months. Disk, who was referred to by his real name, Marc Williams, throughout the hearing, got the same. And one of Ellis's mates, Oliver Brennan, was given an eight-month sentence in a young offenders' institution.

They were all dealt with before me and because they all escaped jail time, I began to wonder whether I would get a suspended sentence, too. I knew what I had been told by my lawyer, obviously, but I thought maybe he had been overly pessimistic and that perhaps this guy was a lenient judge who was going to give me a second chance.

I had support in the public gallery, including my agent Simon and Richard Walker, the press officer from Watford. The family of one of the victims had come, too. The dad was sitting in the row behind my friends. He was staring at me the whole time so I went into arsehole mode: I stared straight back at him and watched him the whole way through.

He was angry at me for hurting his son and I don't blame him for that. I would have been the same. I suppose he wanted to try to convey the depths of his disgust for me by staring me out. There's not an awful lot else you can do in a courtroom and because I was the way I was then, I rose to the bait and thought I'd show him he couldn't shame me. We had a staring competition for about three minutes.

I heard the prosecutor outlining his case. I heard him say a group of students had been set upon after a man demanding entry to the Bliss club had a metal pole taken off him at about 2.20am on 29 February. He said the victims had been asked to leave the club and at the time there were a large group of people outside, including me and my brother and my friends.

The prosecutor told the court it was not known why a verbal confrontation had developed into a fight. He said I had punched a student called Nathan Parton, who fell to the ground and that I had kicked another student, Liam Baister, in the head while he was on the floor. It was the first time I had heard the names of the victims. It was pointed out that my brother had played a lesser role in the fight and that he had got involved because he had come to my aid and had kicked Mr Parton to the upper part of his body. As a result of the incident, Mr Parton lost consciousness briefly and suffered a broken jaw, while Mr Baister had to have 16 internal stitches put into his lip as well as four external ones.

Then they played the footage of the brawl on the screen in the courtroom. The judge saw the kick and heard I was charged with affray. He said he was surprised that I had not been charged with grievous bodily harm. He looked annoyed. He said he thought that the charge should be upgraded but because I had already pleaded guilty to affray, I think the law took that out of his hands. None of that sounded like good news as far as my sentencing was concerned.

They had read out Disk's previous criminal record and there were about 28 incidents. I thought he was going to get time and I felt bad for putting him in this situation. But he got his suspended sentence, the same as Ellis. I felt like they had got away with it a bit and I still wondered if maybe I would, too. I thought maybe there were sentencing guidelines for affray that might tie his hands.

Then he started talking to me directly. He said he was really disappointed he hadn't been able to try me for GBH. Then he read out the sentence. It was 10 months in jail. I felt just the same. I didn't feel angry or resentful or accepting or lucky or unlucky or ashamed or defiant. None of that. I didn't feel anything. I just felt numb.

The reports of the case were all over the papers the next day. Pictures of me and Ellis were on the front page of the *Birmingham Mail*. We were called Villa Yobs in the headline. Ellis had played for the youth team. I had had a trial for the club. That was enough to earn the label. That was the worst part for me because I knew my Mum would see that. I thought about her going to work at Birmingham New Street and seeing the pictures of her two sons on the front of the paper on the newsstands. That made me feel sick.

In summary, the Judge David Tomlinson said:

'Three men in particular were singled out for what can only be described as a gratuitous beating. All four of you, to a greater or lesser degree, joined in but the effect of it was that these three men, who were already heavily outnumbered, became even more so as a result of what you all did.

'At least one kicked a man while he was already on the ground and very probably had already suffered a really serious injury.'

The prosecutor said that one of the students was still having flashbacks. He had suffered a broken jaw and the scars on his face meant that he might require plastic surgery.

I tried to zone it all out. I just wanted it to be over and done with. I wanted to be out of the public gaze of that court. When my sentence had been read out, they led me towards the stairs that went down towards the holding cells.

The victim's dad was still staring at me. I looked back at him again and laughed at him. He put his head down. I told him he was a prat. I don't feel very proud of myself for that now. I can add it to the list of things I don't feel proud about. I said goodbye to the rest of the guys and then they took me down to the holding cells.

For some people, I imagine, that is when the culture shock would really kick in. That was when the reality of the situation and horror of it would be rammed home to them. But it wasn't quite as stark as that for me. It wasn't something I wanted, obviously, but nor was it something that necessarily took me right out of my comfort zone. Like I've said before, this was my world. I hadn't been to prison before, but I knew a lot of people who had.

When I got to the holding cells underneath the Crown Court, I saw about four different people I knew. I greeted them like you might greet someone you see in the shop or at the bus stop. They were all people from Chelmsley Wood. I knew these people. I was part of the same community as them. The truth is, I felt fairly comfortable in that company.

Fairly soon, we were all sitting in the cells, chatting. After a little while, they threw me in the prison van and as we left, I looked out of the window and I saw Disk and the rest of the guys standing outside the court, watching the van disappear.

It took us straight to Winson Green jail on the west side of Birmingham. I was still numb. I wasn't scared or full of trepidation. I didn't know how to process Dad dying. I don't remember being scared of anything. I don't remember feeling anything. I don't know whether it all happened too quickly. I felt calm. We're here now. Deal with it.

We arrived at the prison and were unloaded from the van, all of us in handcuffs. Some of the other prisoners had come to court dressed in a track suit because they knew they'd be allowed to keep that, but I'd gone in a normal suit, smart shirt and tie. That was all taken away from me. Some prison officers met us and took a few details to process us through. There was a guy taking mugshots of us.

He looked at me for a second longer than he had looked at the other guys and I thought I saw a flash of recognition.

'Are you Burkey's son?' he said.

I nodded.

'Makes sense,' he said.

CHAPTER 9

DOING WHAT I NEEDED TO SURVIVE

Winson Green prison is an imposing place. I was going to say 'intimidating', but I didn't feel intimidated. It is just that it is a proper old Victorian jail. It was built in 1849 and you walk in and there are four floors of landings and prison cells that house 1,450 prisoners. It's Category B so it isn't full of the most dangerous offenders but I was conscious of trying not to do anything that would draw attention to myself.

It was run by G4S by the time I got there. A few years after I left, there was a big riot at the jail. I didn't get much sense that there was any particular tension while I was inside but I wasn't really paying any mind to gauging the atmosphere. I wanted to keep my head down, stay out of trouble, serve my time and get out of there.

When I first arrived, I was taken to a holding cell. They do that before they transfer you on to the main wings. I walked into the cell and it felt tiny. It was 12ft by 12ft, I think. There was a bunk bed, a toilet and a washbasin. There was a geezer sat on the top bunk and when I lay down on my bunk, I was aware my face was about a foot away from the toilet. I tried not to think about that too much.

It turned out my cellmate's missus had been in my class at school. We had common ground. He was on remand, I think. He had just got there as well and the next day, we were both moved on. They put me on K Wing, the workers' wing. After the riot there in 2016, I realized K Wing didn't have the best reputation. I read in an article about an unannounced prison inspection in 2018 that the situation had only deteriorated further. The inspectors, it said, found it to be 'an "exceptionally violent dystopia in which inmates high on drugs wandered around like zombies in "a war zone"'. The prison was immediately taken back from the private sector as a result of the inadequate management by G4S.

Yes, I saw people high on drugs. But that wasn't a surprise. What you have to remember when you talk about jail is that there are a lot of broken people in there. There are bad people and there are people who have made a mistake. There are a lot of misguided people in there with a lack of emotional intelligence who don't know how to express their feelings or channel the anger they might be feeling.

And there are a lot of people in jail who are scared. So they turn to drugs to get through it, to help them sleep. Jail isn't fun. It's a foreign environment and in many ways it's a hostile environment. You don't relax in jail. One way or another, you are always on edge. You have to be watchful. You have to be careful. It's easy to be overwhelmed by it.

Sleeping's not easy. It's noisy in jail. You can hear the warder walking past with his keys and chains jangling and clanking. That's not the kind of soothing sound that lulls you off to sleep. Sometimes, a prison officer will open the peephole in the door to your cell and have a peek in and that wakes people up. It is not a calming environment. You don't go, 'Let's sit down here, have a nice cup of tea and go to bed.' Nobody comes in to sing you a lullaby.

Yes, of course there were drugs. Spice was the main thing when I was in Winson Green. There was an epidemic of it back then. It was supposed to be a kind of laboratory-engineered cannabis but I saw from the effect it had on people that it put them in a kind of semi-comatose state. It was also supposed to be highly addictive.

There were a lot of bad drugs in jail. A lot of it was laced with rat poison. The people who were doing it really were acting like zombies. It was an eye-opener to see how people reacted. Even weed, in that environment, is hardly pure. It's not grown in Los Angeles with lovely weather and matured. It's doctored. It had all sorts laced in it, none of it good.

There were big blue doors going through to the main wings and as I was going through them, one the warders said, 'They all know who you are. They've seen the papers.' They walked me on to the wing and showed me into another cell, told me the mealtimes and when I would be allowed to exercise in the yard. They said they would let me know later what my job was going to be.

My new cellmate was a kid from Tamworth. He had been a chef, so he was out all day in the kitchen. I don't know if he cooked my dinner, but it probably didn't extend him too much if he did: it was onions and mashed potato. I'd only been there about 24 hours and I was already absolutely starving.

After four or five hours, an old mate of mine from Chelmsley Wood knocked on my door. He'd been on laundry duty so this was the first chance he had had to come and say hello. He told me not to take anything off anyone and he would come and sort me out the next day. He brought me a toothbrush, toothpaste, roll-ons, shower gels. He showed me the ropes.

He told me not to borrow anything off anybody because the rule in jail was you had to pay them back threefold. He brought a couple of Pot Noodles down because I hadn't had much to eat. The canteen sheet came in the next day and somebody had put £50 into my prison account for the canteen and to buy other bits and pieces. Otherwise, you get what you're given, which isn't the greatest.

I did about three weeks in Winson Green. It was okay. Imagine going to a new school in a rough area. It was a bit like that. I was observing people. I'm quite quick at learning the lie of the land, at seeing who's who and what's what. Because of my mate, I knew people would leave me alone as long as I wasn't a dick and I knew that being left alone was all I needed to aspire to.

I'd wake up at 7am and then clean the landings off and on all day. You eat at 12.30pm for 40 minutes, then go back to cleaning. You get dinner at 6pm and they give you your next day's breakfast in a pack at the same time. You've got to try not to eat it right then or you'll go a long time without eating again. But as I didn't have a job for the first couple of days, I had to stay in my cell for 23 hours.

I know it's meant to be hard in there and I know it's nothing compared to the conditions you might face in jails in other parts of the world, but it was still a challenge to adapt. It was cold at night. I had one sheet. I was hungry. Fair enough, I suppose. It's not meant to be a treat. You're there as a punishment for something you did.

From the first day in there, I started writing. I've still got the book at home. I filled out a whole binder in two and a half months. I wrote about the things I wanted to do, what I was thinking, letters to myself, letters to people who are not here. When I feel a bit rubbish now, I have a look through them sometimes and think it's not so bad.

After three or four days, I was allowed to go to the gym. One of my jobs was cleaning the equipment. The fitness officer there said he had had my Dad there before and he wanted to help. I told him I just wanted to keep fit and do some weights and get out of there. I ran into two lads there who I only knew as The Twins, two fellas I'd met on the outside through my Dad. They told me to come with them because there was someone who wanted to speak to me.

They took me to this bloke, who was a huge guy. Even his muscles had muscles. He didn't waste any time on pleasantries. 'You're a fucking idiot, aren't you?' he said. I didn't really know what to do with that information. I said, 'Yeah, probably.' He said that if it weren't for the fact that I was Burkey's son, he would have chinned me as soon as he saw me.

There were a bunch of guys with him and I talked to them for about 45 minutes. They elaborated on why they thought I was such a fool. They said, 'Us, this is all we know, crime, all that shit. You are getting paid to play football, which is all of our dreams and all our kids' dreams and yet you're in here with us, you fucking idiot.'

They gave me a dressing down that went on and on. Not belittling me but just telling me the way it was. They said they knew my Dad couldn't tell me any more, he wasn't there to guide me, so they were doing it instead. And you know what, I needed it. It was a dressing-down dished out by people I respected so I didn't answer back or give them any cheek. Every word sank in and hit home.

My cellmate, the chef, had been screwing around in the kitchen – I don't like to think what he might have been doing to the food – so they moved him to a different wing as a punishment. My new cellmate was a guy who was in for fraud. One day that week, he and I were outside on the balcony, chatting, when this geezer came up to us both, being really animated and talkative.

In that environment, people don't talk when they are new to a group. They try to blend in. But this guy was really loud. My mate whistled me. He told me to stay away from the guy. He said he was a nonce, a sexual offender. Twenty minutes later, he got stabbed. They put him on the top floor, which is where the nonces were. For some reason, they had filled out the wrong paperwork for him and he had ended up on our floor and he was trying to blend in and pass himself as a normal guy. In those places, they find out who you are very quickly.

I was worried about money while I was in jail. I was worried about how the mortgage would be paid. I thought I might lose my home.

I know it's a cliché but those are the times when you find out who your friends are. My Watford teammate Adrian Mariappa gave me some keep-out-of-trouble money so I could pay the mortgage.

That just sums up who he is. He saw the good in me but he also saw that I was in trouble. I didn't ask him for it. He just did it out of the goodness of his heart. I will never forget that. If I can ever at any point, I'll help him out. Nyron Nosworthy helped out. Again, I'll never forget that. They'll never really know how much that meant to me.

I probably owed about £25k by the time I came out. I had this little notepad and I wrote down what I was going to do when I got out and how I was going to pay people back. Simon, my agent, told me we just had to stay quiet and that every week that passed without me hearing from the club was a week closer to being able to resume my career. Once I was home, I could prove to them I was a changed person.

I didn't let anyone bring Myles to see me while I was in there. My son never came, because he thinks I'm a king. He's not going to see me in somebody else's clothes, moping. It was a bit selfish of me, but I couldn't see him. I know I would have cried. I spoke to him every other day on the phone, I told him I was at football camp. I would normally stay away for pre-season anyway, so I hope it didn't feel that different to him.

Within the first week, my Mum and my Nan came to visit me and that first time. They were in the holding room waiting to come into the visiting room. The prison officers were trying to get people into the room and there was some argument between prisoners over cigarettes. One guy just slit another guy with a razor blade. Suddenly, there was blood everywhere.

I just put my head down and kept it down. Stuck to my regime. Didn't get involved. Didn't make a fuss. Didn't make myself visible. Just got on with it. Mum and Nan were panicking when they were eventually allowed in to see me but I just tried to put on the front to everyone that everything was fine.

And then, after three weeks, they told me they were moving me to another jail. They didn't tell me where I was going. I was taken to the holding cells again and I had a chat with a few of the other geezers there. One was going to Salisbury, another to Glasgow. I was put in a van and they just said I'd find out where I was going when I got there.

We were on the road for what seemed like an eternity, although it was probably only a few hours. I was handcuffed and I couldn't really move. There were eight of us in there and it was really claustrophobic. I fell asleep and when I woke up, I was in Warrington at Thorn Cross Prison, which is Category D. It was an open prison but I didn't understand what that was at first.

It was like a Butlin's, like a big complex with a low fence all the way around it. The guy at the reception gave me a key to the room and I was in Unit C, Room 16. They just tell you to go and let yourself in. There are wardens in each unit and when I had been there an hour or so, one of them came round and said if I was going to run away, could I just make sure I left my key because they were expensive to replace.

I couldn't get my head round it. There were a few lads there from Birmingham and we were chatting and they were explaining to me how it worked. 'We are still in jail,' one of them said, 'but we've got some freedom now and the longer you stay in here, the more freedom you get. You start to get weekend visits and, gradually, they reintegrate you into society. You can come and go as you please as long as you don't fuck it up.'

I was still in Thorn Cross when Watford began the 2012–13 season against Crystal Palace. They had been busy over the summer. Every time I phoned my agent he would say, 'They've changed manager', 'They've changed owner'. I'd read the papers and see they had signed another striker and another one. I was thinking I had no chance.

I also knew it was a possibility that they would sack me because I was a convicted criminal. The fact that they hadn't done so straight away gave me some hope that they'd give me a second chance, but a few days after I had been sent to prison, the club had been taken over by new owners, the Pozzo family, and I had no idea what their attitude towards me would be.

Nine years down the line, the Pozzos have been great for Watford and I owe them a debt, too. They have been good for me and I hope I've been good for them too. They've been great owners for the club. You only need to look at the success we have had under them to see that. Their attitude to the hiring and firing of managers is not particularly conventional by English standards but they have made it work. Similarly, Scott Duxbury has been the chairman of

Watford for most of my time at the club. I've always found him to be someone I could get along with and he always tried to find solutions to assist where he could.

Sean Dyche went soon after the Pozzos took over and Gianfranco Zola was appointed as his replacement. Someone told me Dychey had been planning to come and see me to tell me they were going to give me another chance. Then he got fired so he never made the visit.

We signed 14 players on season-long loans in the summer transfer window and it seemed to me a lot of them were strikers. I thought it was only a matter of time until one of them demanded the number 9 shirt. Manuel Almunia (a keeper) and Fitz Hall (a defender) came in on permanent deals, too. There appeared to be a bit more ambition at the club but I didn't know if I was going to be part of their future.

I would stay up late when I could to watch the *Football League Show* and catch as much of Watford's games as was possible. We had to be in our rooms by 7.30pm and the Championship highlights were on late so it was sometimes hard to stay up, but the idea of being able to see my mates playing made the days pass a bit quicker. The prospect of playing again gave me a target.

The warders were great with me, particularly the guys in the gym. They could see I was a bit lost and they said they were going to work me hard. They wanted to make sure I didn't just waste my time in jail. I'd be on a treadmill for an hour, doing sit-ups and star-jumps in my cell, whatever I could to try to retain some level of fitness.

There was a prison sports day while I was at Thorn Cross and they entered me in all the running races. I think I won the 800m but in some of the sprint distances, I had no chance. Prisoners are fast, you know. I suppose there's a reason for that. I kept in touch with a couple of the warders and I took a couple of them to the play-off final at Wembley at the end of that season.

I focused everything on trying to get out as quickly as I could. I did all the courses, anything that would get me time off inside and out on tag. Alcohol awareness, drug-abuse awareness, offer to work in the gym, anything I could do. I did educational classes as well, taking books out of the library. I read a lot: Craig Bellamy's autobiography *GoodFella*, Nelson Mandela's *Long Walk to Freedom*, Fabrice Muamba's book, *I'm Still Standing*. I had never been to a library before.

I grew up so much more in the Warrington jail than I had done in Winson Green.

I enjoyed the company of the other inmates, too. I had a lot of photos and mementoes pinned up on my wall and they became a starting point for conversations. People had sent me the order of service from my Dad's funeral and I had the orders of service from my Nan's and my Granddad's funerals too. It probably seemed a bit macabre. But it was a conversation starter.

I met a lad called Ricky in there. We bonded a bit over music. He used to be a bouncer in Birmingham and he had all the old-school garage sets. I think I grew up because I finally started to understand that I had had a difficult upbringing but so had so many other people. The difference was I had a way out, they didn't.

I was screwing it up because I wanted to be like these people, but these people wanted to be like me. I glamorized them. In the area of Birmingham I knew, they had nice big houses, flash cars, they could pull out a tenner and go to the shop. And as I got older, I started watching programmes like *Ross Kemp on Gangs* and I found myself fascinated by the psychology of it. I love sitting and watching gangster documentaries. I would rather watch a Frank Lucas documentary than *American Gangster*. I want the real story, not the fictionalized version.

There was a kid in there for robbing footballers' houses. In one house, he was sat watching the game on TV. And just for that moment, he told me, he was able to believe he was a footballer, too. In that moment, he was able to live like footballers lived. In that moment, he thought to himself, *This is what it could be like if I was successful.* He knew what he was doing was wrong but the psychology of it was fascinating to me.

Once you are in prison and you understand why you are in prison, now it's just the people. Now it's just the person and everything else is stripped away. Your position in society, how people see you, what you earn, the car you drive, the house you live in, the pub you drink in, the restaurants you eat in, the people you hang out with – it's all stripped away. All the baggage came off and it didn't matter that I was a footballer. I was naked. I was just Troy. That's why I grew up.

That football bullshit, it's not going to help me in here. Dealing with my Dad, trying to come to terms with the grief I felt, trying to come to terms with the rejection that I had felt, trying to deal with the impostor syndrome I had – none of that's going to help me in prison. I understood that so I threw it into different compartments and concentrated on doing what I needed to survive.

I was released from Thorn Cross prison in mid–September 2012. I had served 16 weeks in all and they let me out with an ankle tag.

Like a lot of prisoners, I understood immediately I was going to find it hard to adapt to being in the outside world again even though I'd only been in jail for a few months. While I was inside, I realized I had developed a pattern of behaviour of getting up at a certain time, doing a certain number of press–ups a day, a certain amount of sit–ups, I had memorized about 20 telephone numbers and I was living a certain lifestyle. It was regimented and there were lots of rules. Sometimes, when the rules are taken away, people struggle.

I wanted to have a couple of days without seeing anyone but I got back home and there were quite a lot of people there to greet me almost as if it was a party. I didn't want that. I went to stand in the kitchen with the dog. I didn't want people there. I was sweating. I felt uncomfortable. I was pleased when the guy came round to fit the tag. That got people out of the house. I think they were embarrassed.

CHAPTER 10

SOMETHING PRECIOUS
WAITING FOR ME

I wasn't expecting to be welcomed straight back at Watford. It was what I was hoping for, but I knew there would be some opposition to the idea after what I had done. I understood that there would be some people who would feel uneasy about having someone who had served jail-time playing in their football team. I wanted to stay but I knew it was out of my hands.

I knew I'd be playing football somewhere, but I thought I might have to drop down to League Two or something like that just to get a foothold in the game again, get a season under my belt, score some goals, win back some of the trust that I had lost and generally put some distance between me and the image of a man behind bars.

I was quite nervous about going back to football. Not in terms of my ability, but the fact that you can get a stereotype or a stigma attached to you, people thinking you must be rough. But I'm not. I was also aware that my appearance had changed in prison. I had big hair and I had put on a lot of muscle in my upper body. I thought people might be intimidated by what they saw, particularly when they put it together with my sentence.

I did say to myself I would never go back to jail, but it was internalized. It was never something that I made a big statement about. I realized I had to change. It was that simple, really. When I came out, I thought it was about time I gave myself a kick up the arse and really dedicated myself to being a better person. I needed to give my life a chance.

I started to live a simpler life. I calmed down a bit. It wasn't that I lived like a monk. I still went out, but I was more cautious with where I went and how I moved. I had a greater awareness of the type of places and situations that I needed to avoid. It wasn't that I shut myself away, but I was more selective about the people I went out with.

I was released on a Monday, and I hadn't had any communication from Watford. I thought that maybe I'd give it a couple of days and then go into training on Wednesday or Thursday. But on Tuesday, I went to get my hair cut at my barber in Watford and on the way there, I decided to bin the appointment and go straight to the training ground instead.

I went in and sought out Zola so I could introduce myself to him. We had never met but I knew all about him, not just as a player but as a man. A lot of people spoke very highly of him. He said I should come into training the following day, but he wanted me to know that I was seventh-choice striker because we had built a big squad.

I'm sorry if this sounds cocky but I laughed out loud when he said that. I told him to give me a couple of weeks and we would be back to normal. I was pretty sure I wouldn't be the seventh-choice striker by then. He said he hoped so. That was good enough for me. As I've said, I just felt lucky to be given another opportunity by Watford. I said hello to a few people before I left. No one mentioned jail. It was as if it had never happened. Football isn't very good at emotional intelligence.

According to the terms of my tag, I was allowed out from 7.15am to 7.15pm I was waiting at the door every morning to leave for training. For the three-and-a-half months of being on tag, all I did was go to work, go home, go and visit my Mum, home, dinner, bed. I worked as late as I could until I knew I was pushing it to get home.

So I'd get to the training ground for 9am, gym, train, gym, chat to Zola, leave. I lost 10kg in three weeks by focusing on cardio work and losing some of the muscle I had put on in prison. After ten days, there was a reserve-team game against QPR. I had to get dispensation to play because if the tag was touched, the sensors on it reacted as if I was going to cut it off and they would set off an alarm that would send people straight to my house.

If I didn't answer the phone in a situation like that, it would count as a strike and if you get three strikes, you are back in jail and you have to finish your term. And I didn't want to have to finish my term. So the fact that I was playing in a football match was logged and I was given the dispensation I needed.

I played against QPR and ran around like a madman to try to prove I was fit. I played for an hour and then the following weekend, I was on the bench for the first team against Bristol City.

The *Watford Observer* ran an online poll about whether I should play again after my prison sentence. A lot of people were saying it shouldn't be allowed.

I wasn't going to be cowed by that kind of thing. I made a vest that said 'thanks to everybody on C Wing' that I wore underneath my shirt so that I could show it off if I scored and wind up all the people who were complaining about me. Before every game, I had to go and see the ref and they checked the tag and made sure it was properly padded up.

It was a little bit uncomfortable, but we put foam underneath it and then foam over the top and strapped it because it dug into my leg a little bit. But at this point, I was so determined, it could have been stabbing me the whole way through and I would still have played. Against Bristol City I came on after 55 minutes , which felt like the first real step back.

We had lost 5–1 at Derby and only won two of our opening seven games, which may have encouraged Zola to fast-track me back into the team and I started the following week against Huddersfield. I had to travel on the day because the terms of the tag meant I couldn't do hotel stays.

So I left at 7.15am, drove up to Huddersfield, played, scored the winner in a 3–2 victory with a penalty in the 87th minute and then had to race back to Birmingham to get back by 7.15pm I just about made it back that night but it was a close-run thing.

While we were in the car on the way back, a friend of mine went on Twitter to see what people were saying about me scoring. The comments had gone full circle. A few days earlier, people had been demanding that the club should get rid of me. Now they were saying that I was great and the club desperately needed me. People can be fickle.

The goal made me feel like I was back. It wasn't a great feeling because it was only the start of what I wanted to achieve. It was just a first step. I felt like I needed to make a statement. I needed to beat my previous best tally for number of goals scored in a season at Watford, which was 12. I was determined to do that and I just hit the ground running.

I didn't score in the next game, against Charlton, but I did score against Middlesbrough in the game after that. I got one against Leeds in a 6–1 win at Elland Road in November, I scored the winner against Wolves in the next match, and one at Blackpool in the match after that, and one against Sheffield Wednesday in the match after that, and two against Barnsley in the match after that and one against Hull in the match after that. Seven goals in six games on the spin. It was just about the best goalscoring run I'd ever been on.

Plenty of it was down to Zola. I got on well with him. He's quality. He still texts me now. He is a proper, genuine football nice guy. He is the one I attribute all the goals to. Before him, I wasn't a goalscorer. I know this sounds really basic but he is the one who taught me to shoot properly. He was a wonderfully gifted technical player in his day and he tried to pass on what he knew to me.

My technique was limited. When I was preparing to shoot, I used to run and take two big steps to kick it as hard as I could. Zola said 'No, take seven little steps and pass the shot'. What? I didn't get it. Every day for six or seven weeks, he stayed out with me after training. Twenty balls or more, practising shooting. He explained that the way he wanted me to do it gives you more control.

He said I had the power so why was I just lashing it every time? We worked on different angles and shooting techniques. It was about accuracy and getting curve and dip. I worked on it religiously. The style of my goals changed too. Before, it was all brute force, headers, volleys. Now, I was scoring chips and curlers. He was a huge influence on me to take my game to a new level.

If Zola hadn't put the time into improving me, I would have had a season in the Premier League at best if I was lucky. I wouldn't have survived. It was an education being around him. Every Friday, he would challenge anyone who was up for it to a free kick competition where you set up the mannequins in a wall, had five balls each and whoever scored the most was the winner. He said he'd give £50 to anyone who beat him. In 18 months, I never saw him lose once.

As the end of the season approached, we were right in the shake-up for promotion. We had some good players. The Pozzos had used their network of clubs to make some clever signings and we had nine players on loan from Udinese and Granada. We had Manuel Almunia in goal and Fernando Forestieri, who was one of the Udinese loanees in midfield and Matěj Vydra, who was named the Football League Player of the Year that season, alongside me up front.

On the last day of the season, we knew that if Hull didn't beat Cardiff, who were going up as champions, then we would be promoted if we beat Leeds at Vicarage Road. Hull and Cardiff drew in the end but we suffered a few setbacks in our game and we couldn't quite get the job done.

Almunia was injured in the warm-up that day and so he was replaced by Jonathan Bond in goal. Then Jonathan was injured in a collision with one of our defenders and had to be carried off. Jack Bonham, a 19 year old who had come through the academy, came on in Jonathan's place but all the changes unsettled us.

I was so pumped up for the game. Too pumped up, really. I was like Paul Gascoigne before that FA Cup final against Nottingham Forest when he took out Gary Charles and injured himself as well. There was a moment in the first half when I thought we should have had a penalty and when the ref didn't give it, I was so angry that I smashed someone in a tackle and got a yellow card.

Then Michael Brown, who knew how to handle himself on a football pitch and wasn't a stranger to robust tackles himself, suckered me into a challenge. I barely touched him but he rolled around as if he had been smacked with a mallet. I got another yellow card and was sent off.

Our game was 1–1 at that point and not long after I was sent off, the news filtered through that Cardiff had equalized against Hull. We needed one goal to be promoted to the Premier League. Being reduced to ten men didn't help but we went after it anyway and in the last minute of normal time got caught on the counter-attack.

Ross McCormack lobbed our replacement goalie and he couldn't quite keep it out. We lost the game 2–1, Hull were promoted and we were in the play-offs.

I was public enemy number one again then. Some commentators were saying that I had let the side down and that I had probably cost the club promotion twice over, once by missing a crucial part of the Leeds game and again because I would have to miss the first leg of the play-off against Leicester City.

It was fairly obvious to me that people were thinking that I couldn't be trusted. I worked the first leg for Sky and Leicester beat us 1–0 with a late goal from David Nugent. At the end of the broadcast, the presenter asked me what the score was going to be in the second leg. I said: 'It'll be a different story because I'm back.' I knew that that year, the stars had aligned and I was going to make an impact no matter what.

And so we took them back to Vicarage Road. Leicester had a good team. Kasper Schmeichel was in nets and they had Wes Morgan and Michael Keane in central defence and Dave Nugent up front. Their bench wasn't bad, either: those future Premier League goal machines Harry Kane and Jamie Vardy were on it that day. But we were still confident we could turn things around and go through on aggregate.

Wes Morgan and Michael Keane have gone on to have great careers but I bullied them both that day. Any ball that came up top was mine. Vydra scored a great first goal when he volleyed in a ball that dropped over his shoulder and I set up his second goal. Nugent had scored as well so the scores were level at 2–2 on aggregate when they won a penalty in time added on at the end of stoppage time.

Anthony Knockaert had had a good game for them but he took a dive when Marco Cassetti challenged him to win the penalty and the referee bought it. Normally, Nugent takes the pens for Leicester and he tends not to miss. But even though he wasn't Leicester's regular penalty taker, Knockaert had so much adrenaline going through him that he insisted on taking the kick himself.

When they got the pen, I thought it was over. I was talking to Wes on the halfway line. I was saying I was gutted it was happening like this. It seemed like a cruel way for it to end, losing because of a dodgy penalty. Knockaert took it with his left foot. It was a terrible penalty. He hit too close to Almunia who saved it with his trailing leg. Knockaert pounced on the rebound and I thought he was going to slot it in but Almunia saved that, too.

I was thinking, *What the hell is happening here?* It was bedlam. The ball ran loose and Cassetti cleared it like an angry dad kicking a ball away and it went high, high into the air. I still hadn't moved. I was still on the halfway line, trying to process what had happened. Then something inside me went 'run'.

When the ball came down, it had snow on it but Ikechi Anya took it down on the run with an incredible first touch that killed it dead. Anya took the ball on for 20 yards as Leicester's players tried to get back and then slipped a ball into the inside-right channel for Forestieri. He took a touch, looked up and hit a deep cross to the back post towards Jonathan Hogg, who had come on as a substitute towards the end of the match. Schmeichel came out but he never looked like claiming the cross. Instead, he tried to get in Hoggy's face but Hoggy didn't try to score with the header. He had seen me arriving on the edge of the area and he nodded it down into my path.

I saw Vydra moving towards it but I shouted 'Troy's'. He leaped out of the way and I hit it. Kasper was out of position and so there was a big gap there. It was the clearest my mind has ever been when the ball sat up for me. I just saw this big space and I put the ball in it. I slammed it into the gap and the next thing I knew the ball was bulging the back of the net in front of the Rookery End and the whole ground was going berserk. I had never felt anything like it in football.

It had taken 18 seconds from Almunia's save to my shot hitting the back of the net. The whole place erupted. It was a wall of noise. I took my shirt off and started running and I saw my brother at the front of the stand at the side of the ground and I jumped over the barrier and Ellis caught me. That stand had been condemned but they had opened it for that game for 100 people, for our families, and I knew Ellis was there.

When I jumped over the advertising hoardings, I didn't realize how big the drop was on the other side. That could have been a really bad one, so I was lucky my brother caught me. Everywhere, it was carnage. Zola ran down the line and fell over. Hundreds of fans invaded the pitch. Some of them were lying down on the turf in disbelief.

Joel Ekstrand passed out and had to be helped to his feet. Nosworthy was on crutches from Achilles surgery and he just threw them away. When I finally got back on the pitch, there was my shirt, untouched on the floor. I got a yellow card for jumping into the crowd and then there were 30 seconds left and then we were going to Wembley for the play-off final.

People talk about that moment as one of the most dramatic passages of action there has ever been in English football and I wouldn't argue with that. It had everything, really, from the double penalty save to the sweeping move, the finish, the pitch invasion and the crazed celebrations. I guess in many ways it was my Agüero moment. Perhaps it's the thing I'll always be associated with.

It was magnificent at the time and it's an amazing memory, but it's not my favourite goal. Partly that's because I've scored better goals but mainly it's because, ultimately, it didn't lead to anything. If we had gone on to beat Crystal Palace in the play-off final, then that would paint it in a different light. It would have been the passport to the Premier League. But we fell short against Palace.

And so, even though it was one of the most memorable moments of my career, at some level I associate that goal with failure. I associate it with our failure to get promoted and the loss to Palace. If I were to pick out my best goal, I'd probably say the goal I scored against Brighton at the Amex a couple of seasons later. It was a bit of a scrappy goal and it wasn't even the winner but it was one of the two goals we scored that day in a win that got us promoted to the Premier League. It meant something. It meant a lot. That's my most treasured goal.

The play-off final against Palace was a nightmare. They say it's the most lucrative game in football, worth £120m to the winner back then, and so the club pushed the boat out in the run up to it. We went to Marbella and it was a shambles. We took our families and so some players wanted to be with their families and some players wanted to go out on the lash. A couple of players got hamstring injuries. Training was poor and disjointed. It just didn't work.

We came back and we weren't ready to play. I had bought tickets for 97 friends and family, including those two prison warders from Thorn Cross jail, and I remember every single moment of the day of the final: the drive to Wembley from The Grove hotel, the flames coming up by the side of the pitch as we walked out before kick-off and feeling the heat of them on my face, watching the mobile camera on the high wire suspended above the pitch, watching it even as the game was going on as if I was transfixed by it. I was taking in the experience, but the experience took over me.

We lost 1–0. Cassetti brought down Wilf Zaha in the box in extra time and Kevin Phillips lashed his penalty into the top corner, just above Almunia's reach. The whole game was dire. Vydra got injured after 10 minutes and had to be replaced at half-time. Forestieri had a shot cleared off the line in the last minute, I had a back header deflected wide in the dying seconds.

Afterwards I didn't feel that low. I don't think we were ready for the Premier League. I know I wasn't ready for it. If I had gone up to the Premier League that year, I would have been chewed up. I wasn't ready for that. I scored 20 goals that season for the first time in my professional career and that was a breakthrough for me but I wasn't the main man.

I was a key part of the team but Cassetti had played for Roma, Almunia had played for Arsenal. There were so many big characters and I was one of many. I had signed a new deal with Watford by then. Other clubs had come in for me but I wanted to be loyal to Watford. I owed them. They knew that, too, and they didn't want to give me a good deal. They presented it as if they were doing me a favour but, thankfully, Simon Kennedy is an agent who is good at his job and we got a decent four-year deal out of them.

It was enough money that I could pay back all the friends who had looked after me when I was in jail. That was the most important thing. I bought a new house, too. I'd bought a town house in Chelmsley for £130,000 a couple of years earlier and I thought I'd made it. That was the house I would have lost if Mariappa hadn't lent me the money while I was in jail.

I told myself that when I came back I would score so many goals that they would have to pay me enough money to enable me to buy a new house. I didn't want the kids growing up in Chelmsley Wood like I had. I wanted something different for them. I was proud of where I came from and I still am but I wanted the chance for the kids to experience a different environment.

I was living there with a £60k car and my Mum's house was worth £45k. My car was worth more than her house. I had a big target on my back and I didn't even realize. But because people knew I could fight and they knew who my Dad was and who my friends were, I got away with it a little bit because I was cool.

When I signed my new deal with Watford, suddenly I had a budget of a million pounds and I couldn't believe that. It felt like fantasy money to me.

It was a pretty stellar year, given how it had started. It was a decent bounce-back. It made me appreciate football and freedom but it also made me realize how much I had taken freedom for granted beforehand. Losing a game of football like the play-off final, I was disappointed but it didn't hit me quite as hard.

Because I knew that at the end of it, there was still something precious waiting for me. I had the freedom to put the kids to bed. Or to go and see my Mum. I still got to go home that night.

CHAPTER 11
THE PROMISED LAND

There is a consensus in English football culture that longevity in a manager is a good thing. Our philosophy, generally, is that the longer a manager is given at a club, the more likely are that club's chances of success. Maybe it's a loyalty thing. We point to Sir Alex Ferguson and Arsène Wenger and use them as evidence of the wisdom of sticking with a boss if you want consistent results.

At Watford, in the era I have played in, we have never adhered to that philosophy. Never mind 20 years – at Watford, I have never played for a manager who has lasted longer at the club than 20 months. I have been at Vicarage Road for 11 years and I have seen 17 managerial changes. It is not the way we are used to doing things in this country, but it is the way the Pozzos do things and they have made it work.

The fans might not always have approved of the managerial changes and the frequency of them but they have generally been able to appreciate that there is a bigger picture with the Pozzos. They haven't forgotten that the club's future didn't look particularly rosy under the previous owner, Laurence Bassini, and they could see significant improvements being made to the stadium.

After all the elation of that game against Leicester in the play-off semi-final, things began to go sour for Zola the following season and he was fired in December 2013. There was a perception, I think, that Gianfranco was too nice and so, as is often the way with football, the board went in the other direction and appointed a sergeant-major type, Giuseppe Sannino.

I had started that season well. I scored the winner after 11 minutes of the opening game against Birmingham City at St Andrew's, which was a strange feeling, given my history with them. Then I scored a hat-trick in the next game against Bournemouth and another goal in the next game against Reading. I was a man on fire.

But at the beginning of October, we embarked on a run of one win in 12 games that was enough to end Gianfranco's time at the club and our season meandered to a mid-table finish and ended with four straight defeats. I scored 25 goals in all competitions but we finished in 13th place. That summer, Aston Villa let it be known that they wanted to sign me.

Football's funny like that. All of a sudden, everybody had forgotten about me having been in jail. I wasn't viewed as an undesirable any more. My contract was running down at Watford and I was scoring goals and that was all that mattered. That made me an attractive proposition, ex-con or no ex-con. People will forgive you anything if you're scoring goals.

It got serious enough for Villa to ask me whether I would be willing to get rid of the Birmingham City tattoo that I have got on my right leg or at least cover it up. It's only a tattoo of the club crest but I can see that it might have created a few issues for Villa and their fans. I'm not sure that covering it up would really have fixed anything, though. It would still have been there. I would still have had it done.

It seemed like a weirdly cosmetic exercise and anyway I wouldn't have agreed to cover it up. For me, it was just football. It was business. If I scored goals, they were going to like me. If I didn't, they were going to hate me. I don't think Disk would have spoken to me again and I would have had to explain to a lot of friends and family that it was just business. But I could have lived with that.

Anyway, it never happened but it did have the added benefit of getting me a new contract and I went into the 2014–15 season feeling more confident than I had ever felt before. I felt that every time I walked out on to the pitch, I was going to score.

I also used Villa's interest to try to encourage Watford to reinforce the squad so that we could push for promotion. They told me they were bringing Vydra back and they said they had this kid at Udinese who was a talent, a bit of an unknown, whose name was Odion Ighalo. I'd never heard of him but they liked him.

Beppe Sannino was still in charge when the season started. I got on with him okay, but his first two or three days when he took over, we weren't allowed to train on the main pitches at the training ground because he said we had to earn it. We had to play on a field and wait for the opportunity to train on the nice pitches. It was all a bit old-school. He told a few players exactly what he thought of them. He rubbed a lot of people up the wrong way.

We went in really early for pre-season training in the summer of 2014. We went to camp in Udine in the north-east of Italy on 22 June. It was the first time I had spent my birthday away from the kids so I wasn't in the best of moods and there were a few times my temper got the better of me. I felt we were being punished for the season before rather than being prepared to succeed in the season that was coming.

There was an early sign of some of the chaos to come when we had a stand-off with the club about agreeing our bonuses. It got to the point where, the day before the game, Beppe was outside on the training pitch waiting for us to go out and we were inside talking to the technical director Gianluca Nani about the bonuses. Nani was on the phone screaming in Italian to try to sort it out and the lads were sitting down, staring at their phones, playing Candy Crush. It got done in the end.

I started the season off like a house on fire. I scored after 17 minutes in the first game against Bolton in a 3–0 win but it was evident early on that it was not going to be a normal season. In our third game against Rotherham, our new signing Lloyd Dyer, who had already taken a profound dislike to Sannino, scored the opening goal and then ran over to the bench and launched a volley of abuse at the manager. I'm not easily shocked but even I winced at some of it. He called him all the names under the sun. Lloydy was gone soon into the new year.

He lasted longer than Sannino. We won four of our first five league games and were top of the table, but at the end of August the manager called a meeting and said that even though we were top, we were shit and that he was tired of the players thinking they knew better than the manager. He said he had never had players show such disrespect to him as we had done.

He said he didn't need it and he was going to go and tell Gino he was going to leave. He was as good as his word. We were all looking at each other, wondering what was going on. We were only five games in and had just put four past Huddersfield. Sannino always seemed to find negatives even when we were winning. He was a perfectionist. But when you keep hearing how bad you are, lads will turn away from it after a little while. And that's what happened.

So Sannino left and we got Óscar García, the former Brighton boss. I was pleased about that. I liked playing against García's teams because they played good stuff. With the players we had, I thought I might get a lot of chances when he started getting Watford playing his way. He came in and we lost 1–0 to Charlton in his first game. A couple of days later, they had arranged a new team photo with him in it but when we all got together, he wasn't there.

He had been complaining of chest pains and he was taken into hospital. The goalkeeping coach took over on a temporary basis. The next game was away at Blackpool and I tore my hamstring. At the end of September, the club announced that Óscar García needed to take a rest from football for health reasons and had been replaced as boss by Billy McKinlay. Óscar had lasted for just 27 days.

Billy had left his job as first-team coach at Fulham to join Óscar's staff. He said later he hadn't expected to get the main job. He pulled me and Keith Andrews aside the day he took over and said, 'You run the dressing room, I'll do the rest.' He led us to a win over Brentford and a draw against Brighton in his only two matches at the helm.

We were third in the Championship, level on points with the two clubs above us. Then the club fired him. He had been in charge eight days. He wasn't even in charge long enough to sign his contract. 'I was surprised, to say the least,' Billy told the press about his dismissal.

And so on 7 October, Slaviša Jokanović was appointed manager. The first week of October and we were already on our fourth manager of the season. I read an analysis in the *Guardian* that tried to explain the club's way of working. 'It is felt that Jokanović will better adapt to the unusual role, almost without precedent in British football, demanded of managers at Vicarage Road,' the report said. 'The club is owned by the Italian family that also controls Udinese and Granada, with much of the group's infrastructure and all scouting based in Udine, and the manager does not have the influence expected by most British potential recruits.'

The level of upheaval was unprecedented, even for us, and Gino Pozzo released a statement about Slav's appointment. 'Our job is always to act in the best long-term interests of this football club,' he said. 'There can be no compromise on this – whatever the circumstances.

'I fully support the view from our technical staff that, given the talented squad which has been assembled and our position in the league, an experienced head coach with a winning pedigree is of primary importance to help ensure the success we are all striving for.'

Nothing to see here, basically. Move on. Slav's recent managerial record didn't exactly suggest he was going to be here for the long haul, either, though. After a promising start to his managerial career with Partizan Belgrade, he'd bounced around clubs in Thailand, Bulgaria and the Spanish second division before we appointed him.

It looked as if he might be heading out of the revolving door fairly soon, too. We won a couple of games early in his tenure but then we lost four on the bounce in November and the word was that if we lost the next game, against Fulham at Craven Cottage on 5 December, Slav would be gone and we would be looking for manager number five.

Well, we went to Fulham and won 5–0, I scored a hat-trick and the season kicked on from there. All the chaos drifted away and we started scoring goals for fun. We beat Charlton 5–0 and Blackpool 7–2 in successive matches in January and the club made a couple of brilliant signings, Ben Watson and Matt Connolly, who made a huge difference to us in the run-in.

We had a fantastic team anyway and their arrival gave us more momentum at exactly the right time. Ben and Matty were seasoned veterans who knew their way around the Championship and had the kind of winning mentality that was crucial in getting us over the line in games. We were a nice football team but we missed that horrible hard bastard in the middle, which was what Ben brought to the party. It was a really shrewd move by Scott Duxbury, the club's chief executive.

The Blackpool match was one of the games that proved his worth to us. We were actually 2–0 down at half time and then two minutes into the second half, Ben smashed one of the Blackpool players with a fantastic tackle, the ball ran loose and Ighalo scored. We grabbed four times in the first 14 minutes of the second half. Iggy scored four goals in that game and our partnership got better and better, too. He finished with 20 league goals that season and I got 21.

As the season headed towards its climax, it felt as if we were always chasing the top two, Bournemouth and Norwich. We were third with five games to go but it was incredibly close. In those final weeks of the season, we seemed to play after our promotion rivals all the time, which heaped more and more pressure on us as the prize got closer.

We played Forest at the City Ground on a Wednesday night in mid-April, knowing that we had to win to keep pace with the other two, knowing that we couldn't afford to slip up now, knowing that the first team to blink was going to miss out on promotion to the Premier League. We went on a run where we beat Middlesbrough, we won at Millwall and we won at Forest and we were still third. Every time we played it was like must-win, must-win, must-win.

There were three games left. Next up, we played Birmingham at Vicarage Road and a goal from Craig Cathcart gave us a narrow win. And finally, the others slipped up. Suddenly, we were top with two games to go, away at Brighton and home to Sheffield Wednesday.

At last we knew that our destiny was in our own hands. And the game against Brighton at the Amex was a lunchtime kick-off. For the first time in what seemed like an age, we would be playing before our rivals. It was our chance to pile the pressure on them.

We were almost there. We had done it in spite of all the chaos. All the changes were traumatic in some ways, the way it was one thing after another, the way that everyone outside the club said how counter-productive it was, the way everybody called us a basket-case club and said that it would doom us to failure.

There was so much mixed messaging. A manager would be sold to us and then sacked. It was the unpredictability of it in a situation when everything is supposed to be predictable in football and ordered and organized. But it didn't affect our results. We refused to let it derail us. I think that says an awful lot about the mental strength of our group of players.

What was strange about it was that it didn't matter who the manager was. We had a nucleus of players who understood how things worked at the club. Everything you would say to propel a team to be successful all came from the players because the players were good enough. We blocked out the chaos and made our own camp within the camp. There were all sorts of issues going on, all sorts of uncertainty, but we stuck together and got it done.

Jokanović was a good guy. He was smart enough to understand that the players ruled it. He never tried to enforce any strict changes.

But there was no training session he did that really stuck in my head. That's not a criticism of him. When Slav joined, we were already well into the season and there was not a lot of time for coaching. It was playing and recovering. It was game, game, game. The Championship is a slog – don't let anyone ever tell you otherwise.

When I say the players ruled it, by the way, it would be easy to misinterpret that as a suggestion that player power was running wild at Watford. That is something that has been aimed at me, in particular, down the years. There is this idea that I run Watford, that I treat it like a personal fiefdom. It's absolute garbage. I don't dictate anything. I find out about decisions at the same as all the other players.

It is true that some dressing rooms are stronger than others and in my time at Watford we have always had strong characters there. But all dressing rooms need guidance and parameters to work in. That's where people get confused. It's about common sense, really, not player power. There are some things it is better for the players to take control of and the manager to stay away from.

The players had a chat among themselves earlier in the season before that crucial game at Fulham. It was like a pep talk, really. It was a resetting of standards, a call to arms. We knew we had to step things up. Players can't be late, basic stuff like that. Slav was fine with that. He said he liked that. He liked us policing some aspects of the dressing room.

He added one or two rules and he allowed us to enforce those rules. Some managers want to be hands-on and have fingers in every pie and they stretch themselves a little bit too thin. But Slav was a manager who was also taking sessions and he was smart enough to know that he couldn't do everything. He delegated to me, Ben Watson and goalkeeper Heurelho Gomes. We took care of it and it worked out really well. It was a good balance.

We didn't start well against Brighton. They played us off the park for the first half an hour. Then Slav made the call of his managerial life and changed our system from 3-5-2 to 4-4-2. He took Ikechi Anya off after 26 minutes and replaced him with Dániel Tőzsér. He moved Matty Connolly to left back and we began to get a foothold in the game.

A couple of minutes after he made the change, I put us ahead. We had hardly threatened the Brighton goal up until that point but there was a scramble in their area and Ighalo nearly scored. Brighton couldn't clear it properly, Connolly swung the ball back into the box and it fell to Ighalo about ten yards out. He backheeled it to me, I took one touch to take it away from a defender and then smashed it across David Stockdale and into the bottom corner.

I've said this before but I count that as the best goal I've ever scored. Not the most spectacular but the most important and the most meaningful. It was a goal that opened the path to the Premier League for me and for the club and I knew how significant it was the moment it hit the net. I ran over to the corner flag and gave it a solid right hook.

There were times in the second half when we rode our luck. Brighton had several chances. Chris O'Grady nearly scored with a header that looked as if it had beaten Gomes in our goal. It was destined for the corner but there was sand in the goalmouth and the ball landed on it and spun just wide of the post. It turned as sharply as a Shane Warne leg-break. If there had been grass there, it would have gone in. It felt like divine intervention.

They threw everything at us in the closing stages, with Gomes making a couple of brave saves. Then deep into added time, we broke up yet another attack and the ball was cleared towards the half way line. I ran on to it and took it down the touchline and then I saw Vydra wide, wide open in the middle. I curled the ball round the last defender into his path. He brought it down on his chest, took a touch to get it out of his feet and then slotted it past Stockdale.

The Watford fans behind the goal went berserk. Slav and his staff on the touchline went berserk. I ran over to celebrate with Vydra and a couple of the other players and when I looked over my shoulder, I saw a lot of our players lying on their backs on the turf, totally exhausted. We had given absolutely everything. We knew we had one foot in the Premier League now.

We hopped on the bus and started the drive back to Watford. We turned the television on and watched Fulham's game with Middlesbrough at Craven Cottage. Middlesbrough were one of the teams who could still deny us automatic promotion. Norwich were the other one, and they were playing at Rotherham. For much of the journey, it looked as if they were both going to win. We were going round the M25 and Norwich were ahead. Fulham and Middlesbrough were in a goalfest.

We were getting close to the training ground when an alert flashed up that Rotherham had equalized against Norwich in the 86th minute. That game ended in a draw. Norwich couldn't catch us. Then Ross McCormack put Fulham 4-3 up against Middlesbrough in the fourth minute of injury time.

If it stayed like that, we would be promoted. We all went mad when Fulham's fourth goal went in but then Middlesbrough poured forward and there were still a few minutes of added time to play. At that point, we got to the driveway leading to the training ground gates. The reception is bad there and, right on cue, we lost the pictures of the game.

Someone turned a radio commentary on and we listened to the final moments of the game. People were standing up in the aisle, watching the scores on the ticker, listening to the commentary. Fulham held on. The final whistle went to confirm that they had won 4–3. Middlesbrough couldn't catch us, either. We were promoted. The bus erupted. It was absolute carnage, cheers and shouts, people bouncing up and down.

Miguel Layún, our Mexican defender, was ahead of the curve with social media back then and he posted the scenes of our bus celebrations on Twitter. That footage went viral. I still love watching that footage now. It's a great memento of a wonderful time in my career.

We rolled up at the training ground and I got off the bus and I saw big Rene Gilmartin, our third-choice goalie. Rene and I had started off at Walsall together and there was something about seeing him that brought back memories of another time when so many of those dear to me were still alive. I hugged Rene and burst out crying.

I'm not a crying dude. I hadn't cried for about five years. I couldn't believe we had actually done it but, in many ways, it wasn't really the fact that we had been promoted that was making me cry. It suddenly hit me that my Dad and my Granddad would never get to see me play in the Premier League.

The people who taught me how to play football, made sure I could go to football and got me boots, they were not able to see me play in the best league in the world and achieve what would have been their dream as well as mine. We have all been kids playing 'Wembley' up against the garages, pretending to be Teddy Sheringham or Ian Wright as a kid, and now I knew I was going to play in the very league where those guys did it.

That was so far from what I came from that it was bordering on crazy to think that this could happen to someone like me. I think I was overcome by emotion because I hadn't been expecting promotion to happen that afternoon. I wasn't mentally prepared for it at that time.

I would have loved to have phoned my Dad and told him about it and heard his voice. I know what it would have meant to him. I still had my Dad's name saved in my phone, and my Granddad's contact details, too. I wanted to pick up my phone, but I couldn't. I would have given anything to hear my Dad pick up the phone. So, while there was great happiness in what we had achieved there was also a dagger of sadness.

CHAPTER 12

'YOU BELONG HERE, FELLA'

I'd promised a couple of my friends we'd go to Vegas that summer if we got promoted. A few minutes after the final whistle went in the Fulham–Middlesbrough game, I got two texts. 'Vegas it is, then . . .' I decided we'd do it in style this time. I had the money and so we went first class and stayed at the Wynn Encore. We had a really good bash at it.

It worked well for me. I had a holiday blow-out early in the summer and then I dedicated myself to getting ready for the new season. When the fixtures came out, we were down to play Everton at Goodison Park on the opening day. That sent shivers down my spine. I always thought of Everton as the Merseyside equivalent of Birmingham City. They were the working-class club, the people's club. I loved Goodison, too. A proper club with a proper ground.

All I heard that summer was how Watford were going to be embarrassed in the top flight. There was no argument about whether we were going to be relegated or not. Everybody was agreed on that. The only argument was about quite how badly we would do. There was a consensus that we would set a new record for the lowest number of points in a Premier League season.

The Derby County team of 2007–08 were the holders of that particular distinction with 11. They only managed one Premier League victory, against Newcastle United. Their goal difference was –69. That was to be our fate, apparently. That was how bad we were going to be, according to people like Paul Merson who said we would fall apart.

I listened to all of it and I thought it was laughable. I was thinking, *Don't you understand how good we are?* I had scored 20 goals three years in a row, for a start. I thought that deserved a little more respect. Ighalo was a terrific striker. We had signed Étienne Capoue from Spurs and Abdoulaye Doucouré from Rennes. I knew we were going to surprise people.

Slav Jokanović had left the club in June. He said he felt Watford no longer wanted him. He was replaced with Quique Sánchez Flores, the former Atlético Madrid boss, who was a suave individual. I liked his style. When we were away in Austria for pre-season, he kept me company on some of the runs. I had come back from Vegas, so I was probably about two kilos overweight. I was in Fat Club the first week, doing the running around the pitch.

When you are in Fat Club, it's a bit humiliating and shameful. While everyone else is going off to have a nap, you are going off to have an extra gym session. The clubs don't call it Fat Club, but the lads do. I always used to look at pre-season as my time to get fit. In football now, players always seem to be fit. They're always ready to go.

I liked to have a really good time for three or four weeks and then smash the weight down for the next two weeks before we went back. Sometimes I would make it and sometimes I wouldn't. The first few days out in Austria, Quique ran with me and we just talked football, nothing about Watford or what we were going to do moving forward, just ideas and how we saw the game.

I knew I could play in the Prem. No problem. I knew I was ready. I had played League Two and did the step up to League One and I played League One and did the step up to the Championship so I thought, *How hard can the Prem be?* That was my thought process. And all I heard was we were going to be bottom. It wasn't just before a ball had been kicked. People had written us off before a pre-season ball had been kicked. They had decided we weren't good enough.

There were other things that encouraged me. I had played a lot against Wilfried Zaha in the Championship and I saw what Wilf had done in the Premier League after he had helped Crystal Palace get promoted. He had that false start with Manchester United but when he went back to Palace, he had taken to it like a duck to water. I wasn't arrogant but I was confident enough to say that if I had a good pre-season I would be okay.

Watford sold Danny Graham to Swansea the year after I went to the club and he got 12 goals in his first season in the Prem and I wanted to show I could do that and hopefully more. I suppose maybe people would class me as an old-fashioned centre-forward but I didn't mind. There was still room for strikers like me. Ricky

Lambert had done well enough for Southampton to earn a place in England's 2014 World Cup squad. I thought maybe that chance might come for me.

For me, the Premier League was all about testing myself. I wanted to play against Manchester United. I wanted to play against Chelsea. I wanted to see if I could actually do it. That pre-season, I was so determined that I was going to give myself the best opportunity to perform that I got myself into the best shape I had ever been in.

I was named in the starting line-up for the Everton game on the opening day. I walked into the away dressing room at Goodison and saw my name on my shirt with the captain's armband next to it. It was a Premier League captain's armband with the Premier League logo on it. I thought, *Fucking hell, kid, you've made it.* That was the moment I knew it was all real.

I nearly got sent off after about five minutes. I chased John Stones down and absolutely smashed him. Today, I would have been red-carded but thankfully he got up. We played well and should have won. We took the lead twice and both times we were pegged back. Everton got their second equalizer four minutes from the end, which was a bit of a sickener, but the way we had played and competed gave us confidence straight away that we were going to be able to cut it at that level.

We started off 4-5-1 that season but after a couple of games, we switched to 4-4-2 and Ighalo and I went on a spree. Whatever Iggy hit went in and whatever I attempted came off. I scored 13 goals and had about eight assists. Iggy got 15 goals. We beat Liverpool at home. I scored against Man United at home and scored against Chelsea. I got three against Villa. We never disgraced ourselves.

I enjoyed the game against Liverpool at home the most. We beat them 3–0 at Vicarage Road in the last game before Christmas and the victory took us up to seventh in the table, a point off the Champions League spots. We had 28 points by then. So much for beating Derby's record.

We were a couple of places above Liverpool in the table, too. It was one of Jürgen Klopp's early games after he had taken over. Roberto Firmino and Jordan Henderson were in the side, but Klopp's team were very much a work in progress. They had Martin Škrtel and Mamadou Sakho in central defence and Ighalo and I destroyed them. The first chance I got to go up for a high ball, I went shoulder to shoulder with Škrtel and I won the header and I hit him with my shoulder as well.

I heard him go 'oof' as I hit him, like the air had been knocked out of him and I thought, *I've fucking got you already.* All I did that game was run into him as hard as I could and make him really uncomfortable. He went off a few minutes before half time with an injury. When I played like that against a major team like Liverpool, it made me think, *You belong here, fella.* I didn't score that day but I had a hand in a couple of the goals. It was a really good all-round performance from the whole team.

It wasn't all sweetness and light between me and Ighalo. We had fallings-out. We played Manchester United away at the beginning of March and Iggy was a huge United fan. It was his boyhood dream to score at Old Trafford and for the entire week before the game, he trained with a real intensity. You could almost see the thought in his head without him articulating it: I've got to score, I've got to score.

I knew I was going to play well. I could feel it. I wasn't a United fan but there were 75,000 people inside Old Trafford and it was the biggest crowd I'd ever played in front of. I was pumped up, too. We started really well and Iggy had four of five chances in the first half alone.

Towards the end of the first half, I played in a pass to him and he was eight yards out. He took it past a defender and because I had continued my run to go for the return pass, all he had to do was square it across the box and I would have scored a tap-in at Old Trafford. But he shot from an impossible angle and I lost my shit.

I was done. I was so angry with him. At half time, the manager took me into the toilets and told me to calm down. I was going to kill him. When I was a kid, my Dad told me to watch Teddy Sheringham and Andy Cole and Dwight Yorke so it wasn't only Iggy who dreamt of scoring at Old Trafford.

I still haven't actually achieved that feat. I thought I'd scored there a few seasons later but it was ruled out for a handball – it was that year when they were being impossibly strict and intransigent about what constituted handball. Craig Dawson headed the ball against a post but it hit his arm on the way and so even though I rammed in the rebound, it was ruled out. I have scored against them three or four times at Vicarage Road but I still haven't managed it at Old Trafford.

When you freeze-frame it, the chance that Iggy had, it beggars belief that he didn't square the ball for me. Second half, we played well and he had more chances to pass to me or Capoue – he had about nine shots in the game. Then, seven minutes from the end, Juan Mata scored United's winner from a free kick. I hated losing that match like you wouldn't believe.

Everybody knew not to make a joke of it that night. Not in my earshot anyway. They just left me alone. I had some friends there and I got a lift home with them. I asked Quique if it was okay and he agreed. I didn't want to get on the plane back south with the rest of the lads because if I get on the plane, I'm going to say something and me and Ighalo are going to go to town.

There is no way I could have watched the game back on Sky Sports News on the coach to the airport, then boarded the plane and then got on the coach from the plane to the hotel and not have said something. So I jumped in the car with my friends and they drove me to the hotel in London and I drove all the way back home and I didn't speak to anyone for a few hours.

I was steaming. The next day, Quique called a meeting at the training ground because he knew it was still tense. He called a meeting with just me, Iggy and him. He got video clips of all the opportunities that Iggy had wasted. He said it was going to be an honest conversation, no shouting, no swearing at each other, just explain what was going on.

To be fair to Iggy, he said he was so eager to score that he just didn't see me. He didn't want to see me. For me, if I can understand something, I'm cool with it. It's when I don't understand why people are behaving in a certain way that it drives me crazy. So when he said that, I just thought, *Okay*. It was over for me, then. I let it go. Iggy felt guilty then so he went too far the other way. For the next three games, he kept passing to me when he should have been shooting.

I finished the season strongly and we got to the semi-final of the FA Cup and lost to Palace. It was a real whirlwind of a first year. That was the year that Leicester won the title and the league was all over the place. We were playing all these teams near the top and you never felt any of them were invincible. We were in the top ten for a lot of the season and didn't spend a single week in the relegation zone. We finished 13th.

I was playing in a good team and I had a good season. That summer, Leicester, the reigning champions, made several bids to sign me. I was flattered by that and tempted by it. I spoke to the Leicester manager Claudio Ranieri about it and looked at it as a win–win situation.

I was the main man at Watford and was being mentioned in the England conversation, but if I had gone to Leicester, I think I would have had an England call-up by now. I would have played Champions League there and my profile would have gone up.

Jamie Vardy was weighing up a move to Arsenal at the same time Watford were offering Leicester £25m for me but he ended up staying. I would have played with Vardy in a two up front and I think our natural games would have complemented each other well.

Playing against Millwall in a 3rd round replay in the FA Cup in January 2008. I'd scored my first professional goal against them four months prior.

My first game for Watford was a 3–2 win away at Carrow Road on the first game of the 2010 season. I came on for Marvin Sordell in the second half.

Scoring against Leeds at Banks's Stadium in January 2009. Chris Hutchings had just arrived at the Club and moved me to a more forward role. It resulted in me becoming top scorer for the club and Player of the Year by the end of the season.

My first Watford goal in a 2–1 defeat against Notts County in the League
Cup, August 2010.

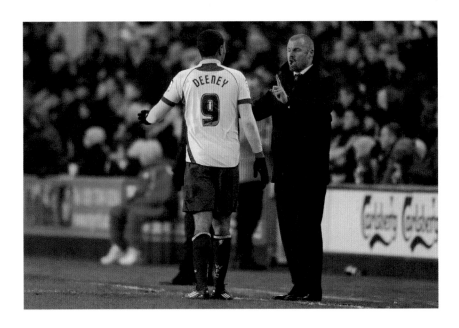

Sean Dyche really got me working hard in pre-season training when he came
back to the Club in 2011. I've a great deal of respect for this guy.

Scoring Watford's 2011–12 Goal of the Season against Ipswich. It was a sweet volley from the edge of the area after taking the ball down with a nice touch that left the defender stranded.

Scoring against my hometown club, Birmingham, in February 2013. I bagged two goals in a 4–0 win that moved us up to third in the table.

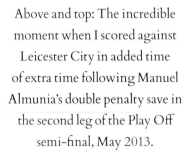

Above and top: The incredible moment when I scored against Leicester City in added time of extra time following Manuel Almunia's double penalty save in the second leg of the Play Off semi-final, May 2013.

Above: Celebrating one of my goals in a 6–1 thrashing of Bournemouth, August 2013. It was my first professional hat-trick.

Scoring one of a brace against Sheffield Wednesday to reach the 20-goal mark for the season in March 2014…

…And the following month I recorded 20 League goals for the season with a goal against Burnley in a 1–1 draw at Vicarage Road. It was the second consecutive season that I'd reached that mark.

Left: With the Watford Player of the Year award 2014.
Above: Celebrating promotion with the fans at the end of the 2014–15 season.

My first Premiership goal in a 2–0 victory against Stoke in October 2015.

My 100th goal for Watford, a penalty against Palace in December 2016.

Back where we belong! Celebrating promotion to the Premiership at the end
of the 2020–21 season.

I knew I had to be realistic and understand that if the move did happen, I would never be able to be part of something that surpassed what Leicester had just achieved. I was never going to become a Leicester legend in the same way I had become part of Watford's history.

Even if I went to the King Power and scored 25 goals and they finished third in the league, it would still languish in the shadow of what the surprise title winners had done. But I think I would have settled in there well. I knew Wes Morgan and Danny Simpson and Kasper Schmeichel. They were good lads and strong characters. They were people I respected.

I did make it clear to Simon Kennedy, my agent, that I wouldn't put in a transfer request. If it was going to be done, it had to be done amicably and with respect. I didn't even want it making the papers. I wanted it to be going on in the background but you don't keep many secrets in this game and sure enough, it was soon all over the sports pages.

I was still relaxed about it. I knew that the worst-case scenario was that if I stayed at Watford, I would get a big pay rise. I was happy at Watford anyway and I was also flattered that Watford were so keen to keep me. I think Leicester got to the point where they didn't want to pay any more. They didn't want to go any higher than £27m and Watford wanted £30m. The move foundered at that point.

Leicester went on to sign Islam Slimani from Sporting Lisbon for £28m and everyone moved on. I don't really look back on it with regrets. I wonder what might have been if that route had been taken but the path that I stayed on has been great in terms of what I have meant to Watford and what Watford means to me.

Would it have made me a better player? I don't know. Although I hated playing for Walter Mazzarri, the Italian coach who had taken over from Quique in the close season, and he loathed me as a human being, I actually learned a lot from him tactically and technically. He helped my game a lot.

And I played with a lot of good players at Watford. Capoue is one of the best midfielders I have ever played with. His ability is frightening. He can do it all if he wants to. We signed Valon Behrami, too, and even though he was coming towards the end of his career, even though he sometimes struggled to train because of injuries, he was the kind of player you'd want to go to war with.

Come match day, he would run through a brick wall for you.

Younès Kaboul was one of the best human beings I have ever met in my life. One of the most dignified people and just a solid person. There's not a bad word you can say about him. And I learned a lot of tricks and technical tips from strikers like Mauro Zárate and Alessandro Diamanti. Playing with them improved my game.

Doucouré was good, too. One of the major things with him was that he had a bad knee when we signed him. They bought him an ice-machine: that's how bad his knee was. But, my God, what an athlete. Every game without fail, he would cover more miles than anyone else. He was stubborn and a man of his principles.

So the people around me at Watford made me a better player. I don't think I would have added to my game as much if I had gone to Leicester. Yes, I would have played at a higher level and it would have been a great challenge to pit myself against the best defenders in the world in the Champions League. But I'm happy with how things turned out.

I went into Watford two or three days before pre-season and they gave me a huge sales pitch about what we were going to achieve and the journey we had been on and the investment they were going to make in the playing staff. They offered me something that was massively substantial compared to my existing contract so it made sense for everybody. What they didn't tell me was that they had already signed an Italian coach who was going to hate me.

Quique had done well the season before but once we got to 40 points, we kind of let the league season peter out and we lost the FA Cup semi-final. We only won two of our last 12 league games, which was relegation form, so even though we had had a successful season, it left us with a slight feeling of drift and a sense of anticlimax after such a bright start.

One thing about Gino Pozzo is that he is always pushing for more. The board weren't very happy with the way people had downed tools and they made a change and got rid of Quique. In the same way they had bounced from nice-guy Zola to sergeant major Sannino, now they went from nice-guy Quique to get the biggest bastard they could find.

Mazzarri loathed me because he had to be the biggest ego. I had had four really good seasons in a row and was a fan favourite and

I think he just got tired of hearing 'Troy this' or 'Deeney that'. He got tired of hearing my name. We never had a big fall out, but he would do annoying things like he would tell Miguel Britos, one of our defenders, to tell me something – instead of him telling me himself. He would try to create division and frustration. He wasn't a nice individual.

There were still some things I admired about him. His tactics and his planning were meticulous. We played Arsenal at The Emirates at the end of January and the day before the game, we went through his usual routine, which was to do a walk through the shape of the team in the conference room of whatever hotel it was that we were staying in.

It must have seemed very strange to anyone who was watching and not knowing what was going on. It was like line-dancing in slow motion. The lads laughed about it and I think we all felt a bit embarrassed. *What the fuck do we look like*, someone would always say.

But it actually worked. It was very clever. Arsenal still had a very talented team back then. They started with Aaron Ramsey, Alexis Sánchez and Mesut Özil but Mazzarri's tactics were spot on. As we were doing shape in the conference room, Mazzarri micro-managed every scenario. He would grab one of the players and say, 'When Sánchez gets the ball here, you do this,' showing his body shape.

'You put your right foot here and when he does that, you do this.' He went through the minutiae of everything. He spoke to us a bit like he was talking to his kids, but in the first half, Kaboul and I scored two goals in three minutes before Arsenal had a chance to settle. We were 2–0 up and we could have been 9–0 up.

It was uncanny how Mazzarri had predicted everything that Arsenal would do and the way they would do it. It was perfect. Not only did he know what he was talking about but it was the way it all fell into place. It was one of those days where everything Mazzarri did worked. It was a bit like the way Roberto Mancini ran the Italy–England game in the final of Euro 2020. It was a masterclass.

Even though I started considerably fewer games in that 2016–17 season, I still scored 10 goals, but I was the only Watford player to get into double figures. It wasn't nearly as enjoyable a season and we flirted with relegation towards the end of it, losing seven of the last eight games. We finished in 17th place, one clear of the drop zone.

The last game of that season, we played Man City and we were just about safe. Mazzarri had put me on the bench for most of the games in that part of the campaign but when we played City, we had loads of injuries and we only had 14 fit players available. He put two goalkeepers on the bench and padded it out with youth-team players. And I still didn't start. It was a final 'screw you' gesture.

I think he already knew he had been sacked by then. We were 5–0 down in the second half before he put me on. That was the kind of thing he did. I think he did it just to assert his power. When you look back at it, it was so petty it was actually quite funny, but at the time it infuriated me.

I still remember how he out-thought Wenger, though. I loved

Wenger but Mazzarri made him look like he hadn't got a clue. It was a shame his man-management was so poor because he had a lot to offer in many other ways. Mazzarri went at the end of the season. He had rubbed a lot of people up the wrong way, not just me. He had made too many enemies.

CHAPTER 13

ALL THE WAY TO WEMBLEY

A new season and a new manager. I was used to that by now. The latest man through the revolving door was Marco Silva, who had a big reputation that, on the face of it, did not appear to be backed up by achievements. He was fresh from getting Hull City relegated at the end of the 2016–17 season, but he escaped criticism for that because people said they were destined to go down anyway. They went down but he rose.

I wasn't around too much at the start of his time at the club. I got a hernia. They're underrated, in my opinion. It was the most painful injury – if you can call it an injury – that I've had in my whole career. I got it checked out by a consultant who was a matter-of-fact older German lady who told me to drop my trousers as soon as I got in the room. She was prodding around my balls and it was so painful it made me cry. Twice. She looked at me like I was being a big baby.

I had tried to play on for a while but I couldn't kick the ball properly. I had no power. And so the day after the consultation, I had surgery. That put me behind the other lads for quite a while in terms of my fitness at the start of that 2017–18 season. I felt like I was chasing my tail.

Even when I did get back to full fitness, I don't think Silva rated me too highly. I rated him, actually, but he didn't rate me. He was a good coach and his staff knew their roles well, training was excellent and varied. He wasn't vindictive to me or anything like that. The opposite, really. I had nothing but good to say about his coaching.

But he wanted a fast striker and so I wasn't really his thing. I was left on the bench a lot – I didn't get to be in the starting line-up in a Premier League game until the end of September. They brought in Andre Gray from Burnley that August and I got the impression that if it were purely up to Silva, he would have moved me on if he could have found a buyer. In the end, he moved on before he had time to get rid of me.

Midway through the season, there were persistent rumours that Everton wanted him as their next manager after they had parted company with Ronald Koeman. It was also fairly plain that Silva wanted to go. He was a manager with a footballer's mentality: he wanted to get to the top as quickly as possible and he knew how fickle football clubs could be.

I suppose he thought that Watford probably wouldn't be loyal to him, based on our record of sacking and replacing managers, so as soon as the opportunity came, he did everything he could to jump ship. It transmitted itself to us as players. The change in his attitude was very obvious. The standards he once had in training had gone because all he wanted to do was move on.

He handled it wrong. If he wanted to go, that was fine but the club pointed out we needed to find a replacement first and we needed compensation. It turned into a transfer saga. There was one press conference where he got asked a question about Everton six or seven times and all he had to say was he was going to do his job until he was told otherwise. But he basically refused to say anything and his silence was deafening. It just showed how much he wanted out.

Results and performances started to slip and even though Everton appointed Sam Allardyce as their new boss at the end of November, the relationship between Silva and Watford was damaged beyond repair. He was sacked in January and Watford did not try to hide why.

They released a statement, mentioning an 'unwarranted approach by a Premier League rival' that caused 'significant deterioration in both focus and results to the point where the long-term future of Watford FC has been jeopardized'. The following year, Everton agreed to pay Watford £4m in compensation. It was a big mess.

Javi Gracia brought some order back when he was hired to replace Silva. He had had a decent career managing a series of clubs in La Liga and had just left Russian Premier League club Rubin Kazan. He was well-travelled, he was street smart. He had the experience to realize that, in the situation we were in, midway through a season, he couldn't do anything radical but he made important improvements nonetheless. It also helped that we signed Gerard Deulofeu.

Deulofeu arrived on loan from Barcelona that January. He wasn't new to our league, obviously – he'd had two spells at Everton – but he was a special player and he and the new manager made an instant impact. There was a lot of negativity around us after the saga with Marco Silva and even though we were mid-table, people started tipping us for relegation.

We drew Javi Gracia's first game away at Stoke on a grim January night in the Potteries, but in our next game, we battered the champions, Chelsea, 4–1 at Vicarage Road. I scored the first just before half time with a penalty and then, after Eden Hazard had equalized, we scored three in the last six minutes. Deulofeu got one of them.

It clicked instantly with Javi in charge and we stayed resolutely mid-table most of the way through the season. I could tell we were building foundations for something better the following year. We had a tough pre-season in the summer of 2018 and that stood us in good stead for what turned out to be a special year.

We made the Deulofeu transfer permanent that summer and when we brought Ben Foster in from West Brom, that felt like a statement of intent. We still had Heurelho Gomes and he was an unbelievable servant to the club and a top human being. When we brought Fozzie in as well, though, it felt like we were a proper team with two proper goalkeepers. We had a good first eleven but if we got one or two injuries, we were really short. The signing of Fozzie meant we were starting to remedy that.

We were flying at the start of the 2018–19 season. We won our first four league games on the bounce and were in the Champions League places at the end of September. We faded a little bit but we stayed in the top ten for most of the season. That wasn't the best of it, though. The story of that season was about our run in the FA Cup that took us all the way to the final.

It had to start somewhere and it started against Woking at the Kingfield Stadium. I was doing some work for BBC Radio 5 Live at that time and they got one of the Woking players on the air at the same time. Ben Gerring was one of their centre-halves and was getting into some banter about how he was going to rough me up and smash me and remind me what it was like playing in the lower leagues. I wasn't even due to travel. Javi Gracia had given me and a few of the lads a weekend off, but I had a chat with the manager and said I wouldn't mind going. I like Woking because the Sky commentator Martin Tyler is involved with the club and I have a lot of time for him. Javi said I could come along after all and they put me on the bench.

We had played a few pre-season friendlies against Woking over the years, too, but even if I felt some affection towards them, their supporters treated me like a pantomime villain when I came on in the second half. I don't know if it was because of the radio exchange with the centre half, but every time I got the ball, there was a chorus of boos.

We were 1–0 up when I came on and then I scored 15 minutes from the end to make the tie safe. Ken Sema, another of our new signings, went down injured at one point and had to have prolonged treatment so I started chatting with people in the crowd and the footage of it went viral. That's what the FA Cup's about for me: being able to go to places like that, getting them a payday that will help them survive for that season and probably the next one.

It was a good day. The centre-half left me well alone, by the way. Maybe he didn't fancy the idea of a scrap quite as much when he saw me in person. He was a nice enough lad, actually. The second the game was over, he asked me for my shirt. I guess he had realized by then that I didn't mind mixing it in the lower leagues.

I didn't play in the fourth round but we beat Newcastle 2–0 at St James' Park. Then a goal from Capoue on the stroke of half time took us past QPR at Loftus Road. I did a television interview after the game and said it was a good win because this was their Cup final. All I meant was that they didn't have much left to play for that season but QPR fans went mad because they thought I was implying QPR was a small club. QPR fans have hated me ever since. It's funny how small things wind fans up.

We played Palace at home in the sixth round and Andre Gray came off the bench and scored the winner in a 2–1 win to send us into a semi-final against Wolves at Wembley. After the game, we walked around Vicarage Road celebrating in front of the fans and Gomes got quite emotional.

He had decided by then that he was going to leave the club at the end of the season and he was only being selected in cup games so he must have felt every time we played in this FA Cup run, it could be his last appearance for the club. I walked round the pitch with him and he was in tears. I don't really cry very often and I'm not good with other people weeping. He was crying on my shoulder and I was just standing there, hoping he would stop.

I realized that he was thinking this had probably been his final game in front of the fans at Vicarage Road. The semi-final was at Wembley and so this was his goodbye to a group of supporters he had built up a great rapport with. He got the standing ovation he deserved. That's what every footballer wants, a win and being cheered by a full house. It doesn't often end as happily as that.

And so, at the end of the first week in April, we played Wolves at Wembley for the right to play in the FA Cup final. Wolves, who had knocked out Liverpool and Manchester United in earlier rounds of the competition, were the favourites, and they went ahead ten minutes before half time when Matt Doherty got ahead of Doucouré at a short corner and scored.

Raúl Jiménez put them 2-0 up with half an hour left and pulled on a mask that he had left behind the goal, ready for a special goal celebration. He had a friend who was a wrestler back in Mexico, I think, and it was a wrestler's mask with those pointy ears, adapted with Wolves' colours. I didn't actually see him do it because I had turned around to try to rally the team, but some of the other lads saw it and it wound them up. If you're going to do a celebration like that, you better make sure you win.

They kept their two-goal cushion until 11 minutes from the end but the manager had brought on Deulofeu by then and he scored one of the best goals I have ever seen to drag us back into the game. Jose Holebas lobbed a long throw into the box and when I challenged for it at the near post, it bounced back out to Deulofeu, who was about 15 yards out.

He kind of hovered over the ball for a second, teasing Leander Dendoncker a bit like Ronaldinho did that time with Ricardo Carvalho when he scored for Barcelona against Chelsea at Stamford Bridge. Time stood still and then he wrapped his right foot around the ball and curled this incredibly delicate chip over John Ruddy in the Wolves goal.

The audacity of it was unbelievable. For him to have the confidence to do that, when the stakes were high and we were running out of time, was a mark of what a talented player he was. His chip was so accurate and so clever that Ruddy didn't even jump for it. All he could do was turn around and watch the ball drift into the net.

I ran to get the ball out of the net and take it back to the centre circle. I felt certain we would get another chance. It didn't come until injury time although I hadn't realized how late in the day it was. It came from a Doucouré ball into the box and I got across Dendoncker to get the first touch and he tripped me up.

The referee awarded a penalty but then there was a long wait while it was checked by VAR. I watched the match back later and Martin Tyler seemed to have a pretty good idea of what was going to happen. 'Deeney is the recognized penalty taker,' Martin said in commentary. 'He usually goes for power.'

I had been practising penalties all week. I felt we were going to get a penalty or that it was going to go to a shoot-out but when there was the long delay for VAR, I just tried to take myself out of the situation. I wandered over towards the touchline and had a drink and looked up into the stands to see if I could find the box where my family were because I didn't know where they were sitting. It took my mind off things.

Then the whistle went and it was time. I had made up my mind I would hit it as hard as I possibly could but it's not quite as simple as running up to it, closing your eyes and smashing it. I don't just walk up and think, *I'm going to lamp this down the middle.* I know that keepers have stats about where players put penalties and where your favourite spot is so I have to be smart, too.

I try to pick the square in the net that I'm aiming for. I try to be really precise. It is not gung-ho. I try to hit certain areas. When we do it in training, even if I score, I ask the keeper why that was hard for him to save. Why didn't you save that? Why was that easy to get to?

Two days before that semi-final, I'd practised my pens with Gomes and he saved every single penalty. I took eight and he saved eight. Gomes had the best record of any goalkeeper in Premier League history at saving penalties, so at least that was some consolation. 'Don't worry,' he said, 'go with as much power as you can there and he won't save it.' That was enough to reassure me that I was hitting it well.

So I walked up and placed the ball on the spot. For the first time ever, my leg was shaking with nerves. I stamped on the floor to try to get the shakes out of my leg. Then I ran up and I absolutely rocketed it.

In that moment, I couldn't hear or see anything other than the goal and me. In those ten seconds, I didn't hear any noise. I just heard the whistle. It was like in a movie where everything goes quiet and all you can hear is your heartbeat. I had tunnel vision so I couldn't hear anything and as soon as it hit the net, it erupted into noise and it was the best noise I've ever heard, 35,000 fans going absolutely bonkers.

Scoring that penalty was down to lots of things but part of it was life lessons. I've had ups and downs in my life. I've had a few dark moments. So when you're running up to take a penalty, what's the worst that can happen? You either score and it's extra time or you miss and you're going home. It's that simple.

I don't think about how much there is to lose. When I was running up to take that penalty, I wasn't thinking about what it would cost the team if I missed. I wasn't thinking about how upsetting it would be for the fans if I missed. You could never kick a ball if you let thoughts like that wash over you. I don't think like that. Just what's the worst that can happen? You're not going to die. You're not going to lose anyone close to you. You might lose a football match but you'll be able to deal with that. You'll be able to go home to your family and sleep in your own bed. There will be other football matches.

When you watch the footage back of me preparing to take that penalty, you see the manager not watching and fans looking the other way. They thought I was going to miss it. Nobody had faith I was going to score. But I did what I had intended to do. I stamped that tension out of my right leg and I hit it as hard as I could. Ruddy dived and he got a hand to it, but it hit him more than him hitting it and all he could was deflect it into the roof of the net.

That penalty was the biggest moment of my career in some ways, because of the emotion of it and because it kept the dream alive of playing in the FA Cup final, one of the biggest occasions in English sport. I felt when that penalty hit the back of the net that we had won. All the momentum was with us now. Wolves had seen victory snatched away and it's hard to come back from that.

They did not give up. In fact, in the first period of extra time, Wolves were threatening to go back into the lead. But just before the break, Deulofeu did it again. We started a counter-attack and when I nodded the ball on to him, Deulofeu played a one-two with Andre, glided past Conor Coady and slid his shot past Ruddy.

I could feel the wind being sucked out of Wolves then. We still had to close it out. In the second half of extra time, I was trying to be Captain Marvel and be everywhere. I overreached myself when I started chasing Adama Traore down the line. All I could see was his backside getting smaller and smaller as he accelerated from me. Fortunately, Capoue came over and cleaned him out with a great tackle.

I was chasing a ball into the corner at the end when the final whistle went and I just sank to the turf in front of our fans. We had completed one of the great comebacks in an FA Cup semi-final.

I felt euphoric. This was the best squad we had had in my time at Watford and there was still room for it to grow. And now we were in the FA Cup final for the first time in 35 years and only the second time in the club's history.

There was one sour note after the game. I did a television interview and while we were talking, they showed me the pictures of Raúl Jiménez wearing his mask after the second goal. 'I'm glad he put that mask on,' I told the interviewer. 'He could wear it out now as well, now he's a loser. So, enjoy the mask – we got the victory.'

Look, maybe it wasn't the most conciliatory thing to say. But Jiménez had taken a risk doing what he did and it had backfired on him. You've got to expect a bit of stick after that and I only meant it light-heartedly. But those words unleashed one of the most ferocious storms of racial abuse towards me I've ever experienced.

It felt as if I had insulted the whole of Mexico and that the whole of Mexico was coming after me and my family.

I got about 60,000 tweets. People were saying they were going to lynch my kids and stuff like that. It was absolutely horrible. Somehow, it seems to have become cool to make threats like that with certain types of people. The abuse reached a level where Watford started an anti-racist campaign with Hertfordshire police.

It is hard to put stuff like that out of your mind, but by the time the Cup final came around nearly six weeks later later, I was determined to enjoy every single moment of it. Some people say it is not quite the occasion it used to be but it still meant everything to me to be a part of it. I never thought someone like me would play in a match like that and yet here I was. I have heard about the days when the Cup final build-up used to last all day and it was the biggest thing in the English domestic game, bigger even than winning the league. That has changed now, obviously, with the rise of the Premier League and the Champions League but I still played 'Wembley' when I was a kid because Wembley meant the Cup final.

The Cup final still resonated with me. It symbolized something. I was a kid who grew up with very little and now I was going to be the captain of a team playing in a match that would be shown around the world. I would be leading Prince William down the line of our players before kick-off. I was about to become part of one of the richest and most treasured elements of our football history.

We stayed at the Hilton Hotel next to the stadium on the night before the game. On the morning of the match, I asked our security guy if he'd come out with me so I could go for a walk and just take it all in. I went over to Wembley Way and gazed up at the arch and the huge poster-pictures of the players who would be playing that day.

There were pictures of Raheem Sterling and Vincent Kompany and there were pictures of me, too. I looked up at them and I thought, *Wow, I'm on the same level as those guys even if it's just for this one moment.* I have always appreciated that this moment will not last for ever. I have also appreciated the fact that I was not supposed to get to this level, with all the mistakes I have made along the way.

I never had a traditional pathway, through a big youth team at a club academy. I came up the hard way. I got here against the odds. So I thought, *I'm going to enjoy this because I have earned it.* It felt like respectability for my career, something nobody would be able to take away from me. I had earned every step of it. No one gave me anything. I didn't pay my way to get it. I had earned it all. I felt I had earned the right to enjoy every single moment of it.

It was the best a player like me could do, too, if you think about it. There was no chance Watford were going to win the league and so the Cup final represented the height of achievement for me at that point. After the league, it was the Cup and now we had a chance to win it.

The only problem was that we were playing Manchester City. City had already won the Premier League and the League Cup. They were just a magnificent team. They were so good they could afford to leave a player like Kevin De Bruyne on the bench. They started with David Silva and Bernardo Silva in midfield and Raheem, Gabriel Jesus and Riyad Mahrez up front. I was up against Vinny Kompany and Aymeric Laporte.

I enjoyed the bit before the game started, chatting to Prince William, who loves his football, and wandering down the line, introducing him to our players. I loved the fact that I had family and friends there and that this was their day, too. I did take it all in. But that was probably the best part of the day. Then the match began.

City were the dominant side, but we did have a huge shout for a penalty midway through the first half when a shot from Doucouré hit Vinny on the arm. The referee, Kevin Friend, had it checked by VAR and decided not to give it. Doucouré was so incensed that he was booked for protesting. We didn't know it then but our best chance of getting anything from the game had already gone.

City eased away from us after that. David Silva opened the scoring in the 26th minute, Gabriel Jesus got another before half time and then De Bruyne came on ten minutes after the interval and ran the show. They won 6–0 in the end. It was only the third time a team has scored six goals in an FA Cup final and the margin of victory was the joint-largest in the game, equalling Bury's 6–0 win over Derby County in 1903. We were battered in the end.

They were so good. You can take losing when they are that good. When they are playing that well, we are not even in the same world as them. I didn't enjoy losing, obviously, but it was about respect for me. I gave my best from start to finish. I did my job as well as I possibly could. I won enough headers against Vinny that it started winding him up but as a team they were just on a different level.

I wanted to make sure I treated defeat correctly. When they went up to collect their medals and lift the trophy, I made sure I clapped every single one of them. I was always taught to be a good loser. Don't be a sore loser. You can be angry but don't transmit that, don't be immature, don't be the kid who throws the toys out of the pram.

At least I achieved that. It was something to salvage from a tough, tough match. It was my biggest day in football and the fact was that we had been comprehensively outplayed. I knew it was going to be a long summer, dealing with that. But I also knew I was proud of where I had come from and I was proud of where I had reached. And pride comes before a fall.

CHAPTER 14

FOOTBALL IN THE PANDEMIC

We had never really had much of a problem with complacency at Watford before. I suppose that was largely because we had nothing to be complacent about. But when we came back for pre-season after the defeat to Manchester City in the FA Cup final, I felt that, collectively, we had an over-inflated ego. We had got a little bit big-time.

We probably thought we were a little bit better than we were. What had got us all the way to the Cup final was fighting spirit and togetherness. Suddenly, it felt as though that had been weakened. It was also the first year we had not been tipped to get relegated, so maybe that diminished our intensity, too. It was the first time we were expected to finish mid-table.

I don't know whether you start believing the hype a little bit. We brought in players like Danny Welbeck, and that was a huge mark-up on the quality of player we had been buying so I think we had bigger expectations. Join all of that together and it wasn't a great cocktail for improving on the year before.

It's not that I'm necessarily immune to complacency myself but on this occasion, I didn't have the luxury. I got an injury three or four weeks into pre-season that left me with a piece of floating bone in my knee. I played two games on it and every day it would swell up and then go down. I just thought it was a sign of old age.

Then I played at Everton – we lost 1–0 – and my knee just stayed really swollen. I had a little graze on it and it started leaking clear fluid. I didn't think that was a very good sign and as soon as I saw the specialist, he said it needed an operation. He said I'd be out for three-and-a-half months. That was a kick in the guts but I was left with no choice.

We didn't win in any of our first four games and that was enough to get Javi Gracia the sack. The feelgood factor from the FA Cup final didn't last long for him. Less than 12 hours after he was fired, the club announced Quique Sánchez Flores was our manager again but we went another seven games without a win. He was under pressure straight away. It didn't help that we lost 8–0 to Manchester City in his second game back in charge. It just didn't work the second time around.

I'm not much of a believer in bringing a manager back to a club and hoping things work out a second time. My logic for that is that there are usually good reasons why the person left the first time and usually those reasons haven't gone away.

I think maybe when a manager comes back, he tries to replicate the way he did it before without realizing that a new style of play has been developed and so you are trying to go back to something that doesn't exist any more. Quique had changed as well. He had matured and got older. The first time, we were very much in it together. It was a hugely exciting challenge for him and he was involved in training a lot.

The second time, he was a bit more stand-offish. Not massively, but enough to notice. It wasn't a downgrade necessarily. He was trying to recreate what he once had. The results still didn't go well. We finally got a win against Norwich to get our first three points of the season in our 12th game and that was supposed to be a spark but then we got beaten heavily by Burnley at home and the writing was on the wall again.

I had a row with Quique's fitness guy around that time. The guy didn't seem to like me and when I went out to do some running after the Burnley game, he tried to stop me. He said I couldn't run because we had lost. But I hadn't played the full match. And I was being told I wasn't playing because I needed to get fit. How was I supposed to get fit if I wasn't being allowed to run?

I didn't put my hands on him or anything like that. I just had a few words with him. I just let him know I didn't want him to speak to me like that and also that his job as a fitness coach was to get somebody fit. He was saying I wasn't playing because I wasn't fit but wasn't being given the opportunity to get fit. I think he was a little bit taken aback that I didn't back down.

We played Southampton next and Quique left me on the bench. I wasn't happy but I got it. We were 1–0 up and then Danny Ings got a late equalizer. I thought Quique would bring me on to look after the ball and maybe give me an opportunity to grab a winner for us. But he brought a right-back on for the right-back. I just sat in the dug-out thinking, *What is going on here?* James Ward-Prowse got a free kick a minute later and scored the winner. Quique lasted two more days in the job and then was sacked.

Then four days later, Nigel Pearson came in. I had a lot of respect for Nigel anyway because of what he had already achieved in his playing and management career. It was Nigel who laid the foundations for Leicester's incredible Premier League title win in 2016, which he never got enough credit for.

I hit it off with him straight away. He was great for us. The whole place was in a bit of a rut. We were rock bottom of the league and well adrift. I'm not saying we had given up but it was clear we were heading for the drop unless there was a drastic change.

Nigel was brilliant right from the first day. He brought everyone into the canteen, the big bosses, the gardeners, the kit ladies, the players. He said: 'I know it's difficult but the people in this room are the only ones who are going to change it, no external noises, no one else is going to come in and help, it's down to us. We have got to figure it out. Treat each other with respect, work hard and I'm sure we'll get there.'

It was really nice having everyone there because football clubs can be disjointed institutions. Kitmen might not speak to the ground staff and the ground staff might not speak to the people in the canteen. It was the first time somebody at Watford had taken the opportunity to say every single person here was important.

One of our first games under Nigel was against Liverpool at Anfield. And Nigel said, 'Of course we are going to lose games but look to your left and look to your right and know that that person is going to try to help you get out of it.' Liverpool were flying at the time and we lost but we were in the game. We missed a few big chances and although we lost, it gave everyone confidence.

With Nigel's management style, we always felt we were in matches. He was a good man-manager. He breathed confidence into us. We had Craig Shakespeare, too, who is really good, probably the best coach I've worked under. His delivery, the way he speaks, the way he puts ownership on the players, are all impressive.

Every session was different and his love for the game shines through, just like his enthusiasm for wanting to make you better. He and Nigel really complemented each other well. Nigel's management style relies on the fact that he has a really terrific understanding of people.

On day one, he called me into his office. What a lot of managers do, when they have got someone like me who has got a reputation within the club for speaking out or having some standing at the club due to time spent, is they try to take you on at the start.

They effectively say, 'I understand what you've done but I'm the man now so don't worry about that.' Nigel wasn't like that. He shook hands, looked me in the eye, asked me how I was. He asked me about my family. Then he said, 'I need you to be at this level, I need you to do these particular things for me.' No problem. Then he asked, 'What do you need me to do, Troy?' I replied, 'You're the gaffer, I'm a soldier, you tell me what to do and I'll do it.'

Within 20 minutes, we had an understanding that he's the boss, I'm the captain and there's a hierarchy. He understood that he could be straight and honest and as brutal as he wanted to be with me without worrying about hurting my feelings. With some others, they needed an arm round them.

Nigel's management style with people was good. He was smart. The next game after playing Liverpool we took on Manchester United at Vicarage Road just before Christmas and the day before the game, he took me aside. 'I'm going to hammer you in training today,' he said, 'and what you are going to do is shut your fucking mouth. You haven't done anything wrong but even when I'm shouting at you, you're not going to say a word and you're going to take it.'

He was as good as his word. Early in the session, he started yelling, 'Fucking Troy, fucking run.' I thought, *Okay, take it, keep going.* Then someone lost the ball and he started shouting, 'Fucking Troy, show for him, give him a fucking option.' I started to waver a little bit. I thought, *Jesus Christ, you're laying it on a bit thick, aren't you?* Some of the boys were laughing and saying, 'He's on you today, isn't he?'

At the end of the session, Nigel asked for a word. Everyone was looking at me, smiling, as they walked away, thinking I was going to get another rocket. Nigel thanked me for sticking to the deal. 'I had to get on you,' he said, 'because I need to demand more from everyone else. You didn't answer back and so if anyone else answers me back, I can say, "Troy didn't speak back but you are?"' He asked me how much effort it had taken to keep my mouth shut. 'It nearly killed me,' I said.

A day later, we beat Manchester United 2–0 and went on a real run. We drew at Sheffield United, we beat Aston Villa 3–0, we beat Wolves, we won 3–0 at Bournemouth, and we drew with Spurs. When you go on a run like that, normally, it'll take you up into mid-table if you've been in a bit of trouble but we had been so far behind that we only moved up to 17th.

We were still only a point off the relegation zone and that was a bit soul-destroying. But we kept plugging away and even though we slipped back into the bottom three, we got another result, on the last day of February, which felt as if it were going to give us momentum to get out of trouble.

When Liverpool arrived at Vicarage Road, they were on a 44-match unbeaten run, and they had won 18 straight matches. Everybody was speculating about the fact they had a real chance of going the whole season unbeaten and they already had the league title wrapped up. They were 22 points clear of Manchester City, their nearest rivals.

I love challenges like that. In the tunnel before the game, I noticed that the mascot, who was standing next to me, kept looking up at Virgil van Dijk as we waited to go out on to the pitch. I told him that if his mum and dad had paid a bit more money, he could have been standing next to Virgil instead of me. I felt bad later because I didn't want it to appear I'd been patronizing to the kid's parents but it made Virgil laugh anyway.

We were brilliant that night. Tactically, we got it spot on. We were all at it, we were buzzing with energy and pressing them in the way that they usually press others. We were all a nine out of ten and for the first time that season, for whatever reason, Liverpool could not cope with their opposition.

It was the night when Ismaïla Sarr introduced himself as the real deal with two goals and a man of the match performance. He scored the first ten minutes into the second half when Liverpool failed to deal with a long throw. I let the ball bounce over me and my marker, it ran on to Doucouré and he crossed it for Ismaïla to prod it over the line.

He put us further ahead five minutes later. I clipped a pass round Andy Robertson and Ismaïla ran on to it, advanced on Alisson and then lifted it over him as cool as you like. Twenty minutes from the end, Trent Alexander-Arnold made a mistake with a misplaced backpass, Sarr intercepted it and, instead of shooting, he laid the ball back to me and I sidefooted it first time into the net. We beat the mighty Liverpool 3–0. It felt like we were in dreamland.

The only blight on the night was that Deulofeu got a nasty injury and had to be taken off eight minutes before half time. Virgil texted me after the match and asked me to pass on a message to Deulofeu to say he hadn't meant to hurt him and that he hoped he would soon be okay. Despite that injury, I thought the confidence that performance would give us would be enough to keep us safe that season. I thought it would be a turning point.

Ten days after that, the whole world fell apart. The coronavirus, which had been growing and growing as a threat, started to hit sport. On 11 March, it was announced Manchester City's match with Arsenal had been postponed as 'a precaution' after several Arsenal players were put into isolation.

Chelsea's Callum Hudson-Odoi tested positive for Covid-19 and Chelsea's players had to isolate; and on the 12th, Arsenal manager Mikel Arteta tested positive, too, and Arsenal's match against Brighton was postponed. For some reason, Arteta's case made everything feel frighteningly real for me. It made me realize this was serious. It made me realize our game was under real threat.

On 13 March, the Football Association, the Premier League, the EFL, the FA Women's Super League and the FA Women's Championship collectively agreed to suspend the professional game in England until 3 April at the earliest. I couldn't believe it. In the world we grew up in, nothing ever stopped sport. They even kept playing football in some instances during world wars. It was terrifying. Euro 2020 was postponed. The Olympics were postponed. The US Masters was postponed. Everything fell.

I was bewildered by what was going on. Everybody was. There is nothing that could prepare you for it. I couldn't have imagined anything stopping football until then. Nothing told me life could come to a halt. That was so far-fetched. When I saw that happening around me, it made me stop. I suppose that's the thing: I don't stop very often. I don't have time to think and reflect. I just stay on the treadmill. Now, everything felt so uncertain.

Everything we thought was a certainty was being undermined.

We are all vulnerable, we are all able to be stopped, the world can slow down. Once it had been confirmed that football was shutting down, it actually made me appreciate things. I started appreciating home life for what it was, I appreciated football for what it was because it had been taken away. Anyone who said they weren't scared or didn't have any trepidation would be lying. Even footballers understood that we could earn all the money in the world and it wouldn't protect us from this.

Watford shut down for two weeks. It was obvious by then that this wasn't going away any time soon. The club told us to take a couple of weeks off and then we'd start training again. That seemed a little optimistic, but I wanted to believe they were right. There was a lot of Cluedo and Monopoly being played in my house. I even did a bit of gardening.

It made me realize, too, how often I tell people, including my family, that I can't do something because I'm too busy. 'Too busy' is our curse. We all fall into that. We have got nothing but time but I'm always too busy to do this or that. The pandemic and the break in football changed that for me and, in many ways, it was a blessing.

While we had time, it highlighted a lot of things for me and reconnected me with who I actually am. It was a good experience for me. It reconnected me with my family and the kids and understanding what my role was as a Dad, not just the guy who makes money and throws money at the situation. I taught one of my daughters how to ride a bike, I taught another one how to swim.

That's the stuff dads should do.

Time is the most precious thing you can give to people but when you are in the rat race, you make excuses for your behaviour and for your inability, or your unwillingness, to give your time to others. 'Oh, I'm at work, I haven't got time to do that, I haven't got time to see you, I haven't got time to go there.' I was too busy in my own little world. We are all selfish in our own way.

I soon found myself part of various WhatsApp groups with other Premier League players and captains as the discussions about what was to be done ramped up. By 19 March, we were told that football would not resume until 30 April at the earliest. The date for a return to playing slipped and slipped as the country's situation got worse, but before long, pressure was exerted on football to get the players back into work.

Some people said we were workshy. That was pathetic. We were just worried, like everybody else. We started hearing about Project Restart and how there was going to be a phased return of Premier League football. There began to be some antipathy towards footballers. Matt Hancock, who was Health Secretary at the time, seemed to think it was a good idea to turn the spotlight on us while the nation was suffering.

'Given the sacrifices that many people are making, including some of my colleagues in the NHS who have made the ultimate sacrifice,' he said at the beginning of April, 'I think the first thing that Premier League footballers can do is make a contribution, take a pay cut and play their part.'

That backfired on him, particularly when Jordan Henderson and others organized the Players Together Covid-19 appeal and donated, between us, more than £4m to the NHS, which was being stretched to the limit by the pandemic and the numbers of people needing hospital treatment.

Marcus Rashford won the admiration of everyone with his campaign to provide meals and activities to low-income families during school holidays and the expansion of the Healthy Start voucher scheme and many of us, across football, were asked to take pay cuts to safeguard the jobs of other staff members at our clubs and did so gladly.

I understood the financial pressure clubs were under to resume playing. The loss of match day revenue was crippling and the television companies were starting to get restless about what exactly they were paying for. There were suggestions that Sky Sports and BT would ask the Premier League for a rebate if the season were declared null and void and that spread panic among them.

Some clubs were still less keen on resumption than others. Those near the bottom of the Premier League had an obvious vested interest in making the season null and void because it would protect their status in the top flight for another year and banish the spectre of relegation to the Championship with the loss of revenue that would entail.

In The Netherlands, the Eredivisie – the top tier of Dutch football– was abandoned for the season with no title winners and no teams relegated. The information I was getting from work was that the season was going to be null and void and we were going to aim to restart in August as normal.

But the majority of clubs pushed for Project Restart and those clubs had the loudest voices and soon I was being told that the plan was now to resume the Premier League season, behind closed doors, as quickly as possible. That was given more impetus when the Bundesliga, in Germany, announced it would resume playing on 16 May, the first European league to do so.

I was worried about going back to training. I had a newborn son, Clay, who was two months old. He had been born prematurely and he had been diagnosed with a heart murmur. He also had breathing difficulties and even though, thankfully, he no longer has any underlying health issues, at that time my partner and I were desperately worried he might be vulnerable.

And then we were looking around us and we were seeing some football clubs saying, 'Let's go back and play football, guys, because we need the money.'

It wasn't just me who was worried. There were plenty of us. All we had to go on, as players, were the media announcements at the time, and everybody tuning in at 5pm to see what Boris had to say. The information at that stage was that this was a serious killer virus and it would affect everyone with breathing difficulties and the elderly, and that we could all pass it on.

Nothing suggested that the world was going to open up and yet we found ourselves, three or four weeks into the pandemic, in the midst of discussions about when football was going to restart.

That was wild. Everywhere else, outside of football, was shutting down. Everywhere else was like a ghost town. But football? Come on down, everyone, we've got to get football back up and running because it's entertainment.

I didn't understand this consensus that it was safe to go back. We had a few robust discussions about it on the various WhatsApp groups that had been set up between the team captains and the governing bodies. One Premier League captain, whose views I always respect, was urging a swift return to work because of the financial implications not going back could have on clubs and, by extension, on us and our families. He argued his point well, but I had reservations.

When we had the opportunity to speak to Professor Jonathan Van-Tam, the country's Deputy Chief Medical Officer, and a few other people on Zoom calls, we challenged them on certain things, and they were openly telling us that they didn't know the answers yet because this was brand new. If I have got an expert in that field saying he doesn't know, why should I put my family at risk by going back to work? I never make decisions based solely on money.

There was a health risk to my family. Is my family more important than getting relegated or beating Newcastle or whoever it might be? Of course it is. Some people in the media criticized me for that point of view, which seemed odd, and there was a section of fans who interpreted a reluctance to return as spoilt footballers wanting money for nothing. I didn't care about noise like that.

The discussions about going back grew more pressing. The plan was that a return would be phased: non-contact training to begin with and then, if that went well, a second phase when full contact is allowed and then the resumption of the league to follow. I had a chat with the West Ham skipper Mark Noble about that and we were both clear that if players agreed to that, we had to go into it with our eyes open. Once Phase 1 started, there would be no going back.

On 18 May, Premier League clubs agreed to the implementation of stage one of the return-to-training protocols, which would allow teams to start training in small groups a couple of days later. Some Watford players went back in for non-contact training but there were several of us who still felt uneasy about the idea we could pass the virus on to our families.

You couldn't have a shower at the training ground, you had to take your kit home to wash it. I still felt I would be putting my family at risk. Watford were brilliant with me. They never forced me to come back. I was training at home in my gym but the club never said, 'Restart's happening, get your arse in.' They told me to take my time. I will always be grateful to them for that.

On 27 May, Premier League clubs voted unanimously to resume contact training and as we got more and more information from the authorities and it became more and more clear how well the Premier League were policing the return to competition, I decided, after more conversations with family and friends, it was safe for me to go back. The other Watford players who had been training from home came to the same conclusion.

It was soon announced that the Premier League would resume on 17 June and after Aston Villa and Sheffield United had played the first game of Restart on that Wednesday, we ran out at Vicarage Road to play Leicester on the following Saturday. After more than three months away, three months of wondering if things could ever be the same, I was a footballer again.

CHAPTER 15

TRYING TO FIX
THE JIGSAW

It was great to be back, but it felt so weird playing in front of empty stands. I felt like I had gone back to the Bescot Stadium, playing for Walsall against West Bromwich Albion reserves. On television, they played fake crowd noise to try to make viewers feel everything was normal but we didn't have fake noise and it felt far from normal.

You could hear every single thud, every boom of a ball. If the game stopped, you could hear the Sky commentator talking. It was surreal. There were definitely players who felt liberated by not having a crowd. It will be interesting to see if players who did well without crowds continue to those levels with a full house.

I look at some goalkeepers, playing the ball out from the back, absolutely carefree and I wonder if they will be able to do that when crowds are back. If those people who thrived under the absence of pressure that comes with empty stands are still doing it in front of packed stands, you can turn around and say they are proper players. But if they go into their shell, we will be able to see their worth.

We drew that first game back with Leicester in June, which lifted us to 16th in the table, but then we lost to Burnley, Southampton and Chelsea in quick succession. It seemed we had lost all the confidence we had created with that victory over Liverpool. So much had happened since we put three past the champions that it felt like a lifetime ago.

But then we landed successive wins against Norwich and Newcastle and we knew that if we could beat West Ham at the London Stadium on 17 July, we would probably be safe. We also knew that we only had two games left after that and that they were against Manchester City and Arsenal. There was a chance we would not get anything from either of those games. West Ham was do or die.

We went into it with an air of confidence. I went into that game knowing I was going to play well even though my knee was hanging off at that point.

I had scored two penalties in the 2–1 win over Newcastle but by the closing minutes, I simply couldn't run any more. My knee felt like two bones were hitting each other and the nerves were shooting pain straight up my back. Nigel asked if I was okay and I told him I would have to come off. He thanked me for my honesty afterwards.

The West Ham game was the last big throw of the dice so even if my knee snapped in half, I knew that a win would make us safe. We were three points clear of Aston Villa at the time, but we knew the odds were stacked against us in our last two matches, with or without me. So it was worth putting everything on the line for West Ham and, if I had to sit out the City and Arsenal games, so be it. Our future would be secured by then if we could beat West Ham so it wouldn't matter.

Things didn't quite go to plan. We were 2–0 down after 10 minutes and then Declan Rice scored an absolutely superb goal 10 minutes before half time to put them three up. Anything that could go wrong went wrong. It was one of those moments in your life when you think, *What the fuck is going on here? This wasn't in the script.*

We went in at half time and I was expecting Nigel to have a real rant. But he was calm. He said we were still in it. He said West Ham would try to defend in order to protect their lead. He said if we could get one back, then just watch their arses go.

As we were walking out, Nigel pulled me to one side and said he was going to give me 15 or 20 minutes and if we were still not in the game, he was going to bring me off to try to save me for the last two games. I thought that was a bit strange – surely we had to throw everything at this second half?

I scored four minutes after the interval and I felt like the comeback was on. I could see it had sown some doubts in the minds of the West Ham players but then Nigel brought me and Doucouré off midway through the half and we could not force another breakthrough. The game finished 3–1 and I was sitting there wondering if I could have scored another one. I felt like we had them on the ropes.

The West Ham game was on a Friday and the day after a match, the normal routine would be that we would come into work to do a recovery session and some training before having the next day off. The first alarm bells came when the club sent out a text to the players on Friday night, saying the following day was off. On Sunday, I got a text, asking me if I could come in early that morning before training.

That wasn't necessarily a red flag either. Occasionally, they'd throw things at you about whether there was anything they could do to help morale. It might be arrangements about a hotel stay, that kind of thing, anything that could galvanize the team. I got to the training ground at 9am and went up to the office and they said, 'Nigel's gone.'

It was like being hit with punches. Where did this come from? Why do this with only two games of the season left when we still have a chance of staying up? The decision had already been made, they said. In the press, it was reported that Nigel and Gino Pozzo had had a frank exchange of views about tactics, substitutions and various other things and that had led to the decision. I went downstairs and Hayden Mullins was being told that he was taking charge of the first team for the last two games. It was dawning on him that he had to go out and prepare a training session.

I think we would have had a better chance of staying up with Nigel in charge, but the West Ham defeat had knocked the stuffing out of us. Hayden Mullins did a good job in the circumstances. We lost 4–0 at home to City but we went into that last game at Arsenal knowing that we could still escape relegation with a win at the Emirates.

Arsenal. It had to be Arsenal. I'm probably as famous for talking about Arsenal as I am for anything I have done in my career. Maybe that's because not too many people in football say what they think. Maybe it's because I don't think enough before I open my mouth. But I said what I said about Arsenal and most of it has been vindicated.

It was after we played them at Vicarage Road in October 2017. We'd come from behind to win with a penalty from me and a late strike from Tom Cleverley. Arsène Wenger, who was the Arsenal manager at the time, said the decision to award the penalty was 'scandalous' and blamed the defeat on that but when I went on BT Sport after the match, the interviewer asked me about what he had said and I came up with a different explanation for our win. I was respectful to Mr Wenger, but I did say 'it's [about] having a bit of cojones, is what I'll say'. Whenever I play against Arsenal, I'll go up and think, Let me whack the first one and see who wants it. I felt that when I jumped up with Mertesacker and won the ball the crowd felt: 'Yeah, we've got somebody who can win it,' and suddenly the Arsenal defence backed off. I told the reporter: 'I know I'm not technically gifted like they are, not as quick, but if you want to fight with me, I'm gonna beat you all day'.

When I look back at what I said now, I don't regret any of it. I look back at it and I don't really see why it caused so much fuss. I think it still stands as a summation of some of the things that are so good about English top-flight football and the way that there is still scope for a blend of styles and approaches. If players at the elite clubs are not on top of their game, if their attitude is not spot-on, then players like me at clubs like Watford can overcome them.

What I said touched a nerve. Some people liked it because it summed up the underdog culture of English football that fans love so much. It hinted at the idea that sometimes we have moved away from some of the old values of the game. We all love the beautiful football that Manchester City and Liverpool play, but we love the blood and thunder, too.

At a time when physicality is being marginalized in the game, we still want our players to be physical. A good tackle will still get a huge cheer in a match. Probably a bigger cheer than a great pass. There's still room for that in English football and I think, subconsciously, that is what I was trying to celebrate when I gave that interview about Arsenal.

I still think there's room for strikers like me, too. You know what? I think I should have got an England cap. I certainly should have had a friendly, especially during my first year in the Prem, when I got 13 goals and 10 assists.

There is always someone you can make a viable argument for that deserves an England friendly. One of the most obvious ones in Mark Noble. He deserved a lot more than an England friendly, by the way. He should have had England caps in double figures. If, as expected, 2021–22 is to be his last season in the Premier League, they should give him a guard of honour at every game, for what he epitomizes about our football.

But it just doesn't work out that way all the time, does it? Maybe I was held back a little bit by the perception that Watford is a small club. Also, if you do an assessment of me without knowing me, I am a bit of a liability. If you put me in a press conference, you don't know what is going to get said. You would be a bit nervous putting me up in front of the world's press.

If Sam Allardyce had stayed in charge of England for a bit longer, I would have got a cap. I'm pretty sure of that. It was the autumn of 2016 and he had spoken to Watford about me and there was talk of me being in the next squad for World Cup qualifiers against Malta at Wembley and Slovenia away. But a couple of days after I had been told about that, he was the subject of that newspaper sting and he got fired. That was the end of that. If anybody was going to put me in, it would have been him.

I never got another sniff. I would probably have been among the one-cap wonders, like my old mate Michael Ricketts, but I don't harbour any regrets about it really. I would have loved to play for my country but when I watch England and, say, Callum Wilson is playing, I never think, *That should have been me*. If you build my football life story as a cake, it has got three or four layers, it has got icing on it, it just hasn't got that little cherry on the top.

Anyway, I didn't say anything about Arsenal that other people haven't said subsequently. Maybe I was a little more brazen about it. I said they lacked '*cojones*', or 'nuts'. Other people will say they lack a spine but it means the same thing. They had good players but there was always something missing. They didn't have heart.

To be fair to former Arsenal defender Martin Keown, he knew what I meant. Keown was exactly the type of player they were missing, as he made clear in his reaction to my interview: 'I hope the Arsenal players are listening to what Deeney is saying, because my blood would be boiling if I was hearing that.'

Maybe I'm changing a bit as I get older, but I don't think about things before I say them or do them, so even though I knew where I was, when I was asked that question about Arsenal, I kind of forgot I was on BT Sport. It didn't dawn on me that there were so many people watching and what I said was going to be thrown straight back at Wenger and everyone was going to go into meltdown.

If anyone actually watched that game back, which they very rarely do, they would see what I was talking about. Ten seconds before we score the second goal, the ball goes up to Mesut Özil and he bottles it because he thinks he's going to get smashed.

Özil is a fantastic footballer, he is technically gifted and his touch is sweet but, in that moment, the ball bounced off him because he thought he was going to get hit from behind by a big centre half, he lost the ball, we went down the left and Clevz scored. So in that instance, they wimped out.

People think I dislike Arsenal, or I dislike Aston Villa, but I don't. I love football. It's all I know. Of all the sports, I know players, I know how people do it, I know what it takes to make teams work. It doesn't mean I'm the best at it. I just understand it.

So when I watch Arsenal, I still remember watching George Graham's Arsenal, tough, one-nil, boring Arsenal. Then it turns into Wenger's Arsenal, with the flair of Thierry Henry and Robert Pires but that was a tough, tough team as well. You didn't fancy messing about with Patrick Vieira, or Tony Adams or Sol Campbell or Martin Keown.

Arsenal had moved away from that for a few years before I said what I said but I was hammered by Paul Merson and a host of other ex-Arsenal players: 'Deeney can't say that, he can't do that.' Really? Well, you get paid to do it. And because you have stopped playing, you have more entitlement to say that than me? How does that work? If anything, I am more entitled to talk about this era of the Premier League than them because I am in it, I know all about it, I'm not dated.

How many times do you see footballers interviewed and it is a generic interview, line after line after line? It's so predictable, you could write down what they're going to say before they've even opened their mouths. Fans get frustrated by that, and pundits get frustrated that they don't see the personality of the player. Yet when the player shows personality, he gets shot down in flames.

Why? Are you worried that I'm going to be better at the job than you? Is that the problem? Is that it? I still believe I was right. I think I have been proved to be right because there are not many people who played in that game for Arsenal who are still at the club, certainly not in the first team. I think most people heard what I said and thought, *He's right.*

I've got a lot of respect for Arsenal in many ways. They are trying to build something back up now but I am not sure they will get there as quickly as people seem to think. The top four of Manchester City, Chelsea, Liverpool and Manchester United are going to be hard to shift and you have got Leicester, Leeds, West Ham and Everton all back in and around it, too.

It can take a long time to get back to the level you were once at as a club and that was one of the reasons that I went into that final game of that interrupted, disjointed 2019–20 season believing that we could get the result at the Emirates that might keep us in the Premier League. They didn't really have anything left to play for and we thought we could nick something. We started with Danny Welbeck and me up front. We were positive. We were going there to win.

And then the same thing happened that had happened against West Ham. We made a dreadful start. We were 3–0 down after 33 minutes and I thought we were looking at being relegated amid a humiliation. But then I got one back with a penalty just before half time and I thought, *There's a chance here.* With other clubs, you might not think that, but with Arsenal, there's always a chance.

Danny missed a couple of good chances, and I thought the opportunities were going to keep coming and we were going to do it. He scored in the second half to make it 3–2 and I was sure we were going to do it but there was never another opportunity. A win would have lifted us above Villa and kept us safe, but defeat condemned us to finishing 19th, one place below Bournemouth and, because of goal difference, two points away from safety.

The reality is that when Nigel was sacked, we had effectively started planning for the following season already. I was actually proud of the way we went down because we gave it everything and had a right good go. After the game, there was all the fall-out, some people were wondering if they were going to go somewhere else, some people were crying, some people were not saying anything.

I walked into our dressing room at The Emirates and people's heads were down and there were tears. I looked at the lads and thought I had to go into leadership mode. I didn't have too much of a sulking or grieving attitude. It had been a long, strange season and it had put football into perspective. I knew there wasn't long left until we would have the chance to put it right.

I tried to raise people's spirits as best I could. I went outside to see the kitmen and thank them for everything they had done and while I was in the corridor, I saw our technical director, Filippo Giraldi. He was crying and I grabbed him and told him we had to set an example.

I grabbed him by the shoulders, actually, and said, 'Man the fuck up.' I knew we had to show these players that we were going again in a few weeks and we couldn't afford a hangover. I told him to wipe the tears away and go into the dressing room and sort the players out.

I said we had all made mistakes and we had to own it and now wasn't the time for self-pity. I told him to get into the changing room and I would go and do the press so no one else had to do it. That was the Sky Sports interview when the guy called me old and I called him a cheeky bastard.

I took the media duties on myself so other people didn't have to. Speaking to the BBC, I tried to be realistic about the future, saying if that was my last Premier League game, I was happy I went out on my shield. I had done everything I could. My family's opinions were the only ones I cared about. I told them, 'I'm a big boy with big shoulders and I've had some real-world issues, so getting some stick online doesn't bother me'.

I was frustrated. It is easy to lose yourself in self-pity when you are a player and you have had a big setback like relegation, but my thoughts were with the people behind the scenes. You have got ladies who work at our place who have been there for 35 or 40 years. It is going to impact them more than me on a financial level. They are going to be losing their jobs because of potential cutbacks.

That hit home. I have been at the club for a long time and know about their families, so in that moment the football took a back seat. Footballers come and go but fans and people who work there for a long time are deeply affected by relegation. A lot of the big players move on when you are relegated but there are plenty of people at a football club who can't just up sticks and go elsewhere.

I wanted to stay but I knew it might be out of my hands. I was 32 and I had been at the club for ten years. As I've said before, it was really all I knew. I'd been good for them and they had been good for me. I'd scored 124 goals in 368 league appearances and I wanted to help them get back to the top flight in the years that were left on my contract.

The following day, I was going away on holiday, driving to the south of France. My partner and I were driving and talking and trying to fix the jigsaw because it felt like someone had smashed our life plan. The club had a few ideas about my life plan, too.

CHAPTER 16

'SORRY, MATE, YOUR SEASON'S OVER'

The morning after we had been relegated, Simon, my agent, called. If you want to know how quickly football clubs can move on from players, read this. This was 15 hours after the final whistle had gone at The Emirates. 'I know this is really fast,' Simon said, 'but it looks like Watford might move you on.'

I thought we would have had at least a week, process what had happened, jump on a call, the club might talk about how they find themselves financially, feel it out a bit. I misjudged that. People had obviously put a contingency plan in place, and they were executing it the following morning.

I know, I know. I'm a big boy and I ought not to have been surprised. And, yes, I had spoken to Leicester when they wanted to sign me, and I had been tempted by the idea of moving to the league champions. But, as I mentioned, I would never have asked for a transfer. I would never have tried to force my way out. Yes, it's a business. I get that, too, but this felt ruthless even by football's standards.

I have an immense amount of respect for the people at Watford, right throughout the club, from top to bottom and this hurt massively, to be honest. Did they not want to pause for thought? Did I not deserve a conversation? Maybe they'd say, 'We might have to get rid of you because of your wages. If not, is there a conversation to be had where we restructure a contract?' And I would always be up for that conversation.

Four or five days into the holiday in France, Simon called again and asked how I was. I felt a bit numb. I've been at Watford for so long, I don't know what life's like outside. The chaos of Watford had become normal. I had grown accustomed to it.

Yes, I wanted to play in the Premier League and had come to consider myself a Premier League player. That doesn't mean I think I'm Mo Salah. I just looked at certain other clubs, who hadn't been relegated, and thought I could do the job their centre forward is doing but do it better.

But my main thought was that I had helped get the club into this mess and I wanted to be part of the process of fixing it. I liked the idea of that kind of comeback story. I liked the idea of leading the club back to the Premier League and re-establishing it in the top flight.

But it started to look increasingly as if the club wanted to go in a different direction. I got the impression that I would not be a starter the following season. If you're not going to be a starter, you have to make a decision. Do you want to be a substitute, a support act? Is that all you've got left to give?

A little while later, Simon called me again and said a few clubs were interested in signing me. I became aware of things leaked by sources from other clubs. I felt I was being pushed out of the door by Watford. No one had spoken to me. With ten years of service, the least I deserved was a conversation, a courtesy call. Maybe I'm being precious.

I had a couple of conversations with other managers. I am sure there is another way to say this, but I found it hard to avoid the impression that a lot of managers are pussies. They like to project the public image of a man who is a forceful character and yet a couple of them were fretting because they said they had heard I was hard to control.

I asked to have a conversation. They said they didn't want to have a conversation because they were worried that would be interpreted as a commitment to signing me. I just said I wanted to understand why they thought I was difficult. They ducked the question. I wanted to know why they thought I was a problem. I train all the time. I am never late. I do everything I'm supposed to, so what is it they were worried about?

It transpired they were worried I would challenge them and their instructions. They want to tell players to stand in a certain position and tell them, 'This is the way it's going to be and you don't question it – ever.' So if we're losing as a team, we can't call each other out? Is that what we're saying? Have we really become that scared of confrontation?

Confrontation of any sort is going out of the game. No one can be challenged. No one can be bawled out. There's an acceptance that you can win or lose and it's going to happen and there's nothing you can do about it. There's a good chance you're going to lose if you play Man City but I'm in the 1 per cent of players that say, 'Let's give it a right good bash.'

The best managers can deal with opinionated players because they have the courage of their own convictions and are confident enough to be challenged and to deal with the challenge. I know players who have worked for Pep Guardiola, say, players like Fabian Delph, who is opinionated and hard-working and only says good things about him.

I know Joe Hart and I asked him about Jose Mourinho and he said he was quality. He told Joe and the other players: 'These are the standards that I expect, so meet them.' That's the kind of thing I enjoy, the black and white of it and no grey areas.

One Premier League Manager refused to meet me because he thought I was too hard to control. There were so many excuses about why he didn't want to meet me. These stories about me only training once a week. Those stories are garbage. I train every day. The problem is that they tell me to stop.

No one from the ownership group talks because that is the stance they take and I respect that. But because I don't shut my mouth, people think I must have permission to do it. But that is so far from the truth.

They don't phone up and say, 'We're going to sign Ismaïla Sarr, what do you think?' Or 'We're going to get rid of this manager or that manager, what do you think?' It simply doesn't happen. I am not consulted about things like that. It's above my pay grade. Like I said, I find out about that sort of stuff at the same time as the other players.

I did meet with West Brom near the end of September 2020, with the consent of Watford. In fact, we had a deal in place. I went up and met their manager at the time, Slaven Bilić, at their training ground. I had been told by a couple of people that Bilić wasn't sold on the idea of bringing me in and that he was more interested in pursuing Karlan Grant, who was at Huddersfield Town.

Bilić and I had an honest conversation. He said: 'You weren't my first choice but we're here.' And I said, 'To be honest, you weren't my first choice, either, but we're here'. We both laughed and it developed into a good conversation. He left because they had a match coming up against Chelsea and we agreed to get the weekend out of the way, then resume the conversation on Monday and push the transfer through.

We shook hands. I thought that was all done. I thought I'd be training with the club by the following Tuesday. I was shown around the training ground, met everyone, the kitmen and the rest of the staff, and because I'm local, there was talk about how they had 'one of us' in the building.

I watched the game against Chelsea and they got a great result, a 3–3 draw that gave them something to build on. I was analysing how I would fit into it and how I needed to play. Then Monday came and there was nothing. No call from Bilić. Nothing.

Tuesday, nothing. I thought something was wrong. It was obvious something had changed.

Bilić had backed out of it. Good luck to Karlan Grant and I wish him well but there was a little part of me when they are doing badly in 2020–21 that thought, *Well, there you go.*

Big Sam Allardyce came in for a while at the Hawthorns. If ever there was a manager–player combination that was designed to work, it was me and him, but I'd come to the conclusion by then that it wasn't for me. I want to see this project out at Watford and make sure they ended up where they should be.

The club had brought in a new manager, Vladimir Ivić, in pre-season. He was a Serb, signed from Maccabi Tel Aviv, and I went to him and I said I was prepared for him to give someone else the captain's armband if he thought I was going to be sold. I didn't want to stand in the way of the club making a fresh start with a new leader on the pitch. He said he wanted to wait to see how things went.

There was a group of eight or nine players at Watford, including me, who had been told that we would be sold and that we weren't part of the club's plans for the 2020–21 season in the Championship. Capoue was in that group, Sarr, Doucouré, and several others. The season started and I was still going to the training ground but those of us in that group of eight or nine went in at a different time to the first-team squad so there would be no mixing between us.

Ivić and I never had any problems. Not until the end, anyway. But I didn't particularly warm to his management style. I don't think anyone did. He tried to restrict everything. No one was allowed phones, which is fine up to a point but there comes a time when you might need to speak to your family after training. He was immovable about that.

He also introduced a rule where you had to stay an hour and a half after training. Again, that sounds okay in principle. And I understand that objecting to it makes me sound like a spoilt footballer. But there comes a point as a footballer when you have done everything you can do at training. What you need is to go home and rest.

So training would finish at around 1.30pm and people would have to sit around until 3 or 4pm just for the sake of it. That starts to become tedious, particularly when you are not winning.

In terms of match analysis, he dissected everything, right down to the minutiae. He walked us through every move in freeze-frame. He would take 45 minutes to get through seven or eight clips. You'd come out of the room and someone would turn to you and say, 'God, I'm shit.' He made you feel terrible about yourself. When you won, you'd do 40 minutes on the things you did wrong and a couple of minutes on the goals we scored.

With the lockdown and everything, people weren't enjoying their football and it became more and more oppressive. We have got the best job in the world, getting paid a small fortune to play football and we work four or five hours a day and you've got a person who makes you feel like you're not good enough to be there and you're doing everything wrong.

It was the first time in 13 years that I have never learned anything from a manager. Sometimes, some of it just feels very basic. It should not be that hard to instil confidence into players. It's not rocket science. Give them a bit of praise now and again. Help them to play with belief. Ivić didn't do that and we suffered as a result.

There were extenuating circumstances, sure. The environment he was working in probably didn't help. Watford are known for sacking managers so why would he try and get close to anybody? Why would he bother trusting anyone? He probably figured he wasn't going to be around long enough for it to be worth his while to build a relationship with anyone.

We weren't playing great at the time when I was finally rehabilitated and brought back into the squad, but he picked me on the bench a few times and then I started against Preston at the end of November and I scored a penalty in a 4–1 win. Ivić didn't say anything after the game but I got the feeling he was thinking, *Oh shit, he did well.* I wouldn't say they wanted me to fail but something didn't sit right with the way he acted.

Six days before Christmas, we had a game at Huddersfield. I trained all week with no problems. I'd scored in each of the previous three games, and I was in good form again after the strange start to my season. The day before the game, I got in an hour before training and Simon called me to ask if I was injured. I didn't know what he was talking about.

Simon said he had had a message from Scott Duxbury saying that he was gutted I was injured and that I wouldn't be playing against

Huddersfield. He said I wasn't starting because the manager said I was injured. I went up to see Scott and told him I wasn't injured. He said there must have been a misunderstanding and they would tell the manager I was fit. I was puzzled by it. It was weird.

We went out to train and the bibs were handed out and it was clear I was going to be on the bench the next day. I wasn't happy but there were no issues. I was doing defensive set pieces and I gave 100 per cent, as if I was starting. After training, we went in and did a bit in the gym for an hour.

There was about half an hour to go before we left to get on the bus for the drive north. I'd started a ten-minute session on a machine that applies heat to your Achilles tendon when someone came in and told me that Ivić wanted to see me in his office. I told him I had five minutes left on the machine and then I'd be straight there. After the treatment ended, I went straight upstairs to see him. I went to his office and he wasn't there.

I had a quick shower and ran over to the canteen to get a quick bite to eat and Ivić was just walking out to get on the bus. He didn't say anything. He didn't call me over. I thought it couldn't have been anything particularly important and that he'd probably speak to me when we got to the hotel in Leeds, where we were staying for the Huddersfield game.

We got there and I sat in the lobby for a few hours and there was still nothing from him. We got up to go to dinner and the club's new director of football, Cristiano Giaretta, asked me if I was avoiding the manager. I shook my head and asked if there was a problem. There was no problem, he said, but he thought I was avoiding the manager.

I told him what had happened. I told him I'd been to look for him at the training ground and that I'd seen him a couple of times and he hadn't said anything. I said I didn't want to start begging to play in the game. He's made his decision and that's fine. There's no issue. We left it at that.

The journey to the game was uneventful. I was on the bench. No problem. We were 2–0 down at half time. I thought I'd be coming on. There was a fitness guy who used to come and give you a couple of minutes' warning if you were coming on. He went straight to Stipe Perica, one of our other strikers, and told him to get ready.

He got other players to warm up and I looked at Nate Chalobah. Nate said his knee was playing up so the manager had told him that unless he was needed, he wasn't coming on. He hadn't said anything like that to me but the only two not warming up were Nate and me. We lost 2–0 and I never got off the bench. I sucked it up. His decision. He's the boss.

We went back into the changing room. Ivić walked round and shook everybody's hand. He got to me and just walked past. He made a point of ignoring me. So I thought, *Okay, there's a real problem here.* The football stuff is fine, I can take that, but don't just ignore me as a human being. Ben Foster asked if something had happened. I said nothing but I told him that on Monday, Ivić and I would be having a serious conversation.

I got in my car to go home and my phone started going mad. My Mum called me. She said, 'Son, what have you done? The radio is saying you were left out for disciplinary reasons.' I messaged our media guy and asked him to send me the transcript of the manager's press conference because I thought it might have been taken out of context.

I read it and thought, *Cheeky bastard*. He had played a team he thought would win and he lost. Now he was hiding behind this smokescreen of a disciplinary issue to try to deflect from his mistake. He had told the media I had been left out for a disciplinary reason but that he wouldn't answer any questions on it. He could have just said I'd played a lot of games. I thought it was out of order. He was trying to throw me under the bus.

The chairman phoned and said they knew there wasn't a disciplinary reason. I asked what was going on. I wasn't going to sit there and take it. The chairman said they'd support me. I said, 'Support me over what?' It turned out Ivić thought I had refused to come and see him when I was on the treatment machine, but I still didn't quite understand what his problem was.

He had had loads of opportunities to ask for a word. The bus journey from Watford to Huddersfield isn't exactly ten minutes round the corner. Anyway, I was fuming about it. It was hard to take because there was no disciplinary issue, and I hadn't done anything wrong. If I'd brought it on myself, fine, but that really wasn't the case here.

By 8.30pm, there was an announcement that Ivić had been

sacked. It said the club was standing by me. That made it look as if Ivić had lost some sort of power struggle with me and decided to quit because of it. It even looked bad to me. It tied into the narrative about me being some power-crazed player. People started saying I epitomized what was wrong with the club.

The truth is, it was a relief when he left. I didn't have anything to do with it, but I wasn't sorry to see him go. Football was a joyless experience when he was in charge. The club appointed Xisco Muñoz, who had had a decent playing career in Spain, as his successor and he lifted the place straight away. He'd been set a low bar so the improvement was instantaneous. He let us have our phones back, for a start. That didn't do any harm.

Ivić seemed not to like footballers but Xisco is a good man-manager. He took the pressure off us and put things in perspective. He has played at a high level, so he knows what it's like. He sat us all down and pointed out that we were all people who were largely free of financial concerns, we had families who were well and so why the hell were we stressing about football. It's sport. It happens. Enjoy it.

In his first training session, we did the perfect footballers' drill: a ten-minute warm-up, rondos, small-sided games. It was a huge relief. An hour and a half of high intensity, good work and then see you later. Football felt like fun again. Like I said, it wasn't rocket science.

Xisco was exactly what we needed after we had been relegated, not the negativity that Ivić brought. He changed our style and our mentality as much as he could between games and the club was buzzing again after five months of being in what felt like cold storage.

At Watford, just like at a lot of other clubs, the canteen and the kit department are the life and soul of the place and if you can get them up and bubbling then you are on the right road. Linda in the kit room got the music blaring again, singing along to Magic FM, and everybody started enjoying themselves again. The whole atmosphere in the place picked up.

Results picked up, too. We could all sense the improvement. There was optimism around the place again. We were still in and around the play-off places and I felt sure that we could put a run together and have a real go at getting automatic promotion. We had the talent to do that and now we had a manager who was starting to get the best out of us.

I liked what I saw of Xisco immediately. He is warm, still relatively young so he understands the players' perspective, he is open to conversation, open to dialogue. What frustrates me is people like Ivić, who have never played in this league and are ignorant of it. Xisco wasn't like that. Right from the start, he made it clear he wanted to learn.

He changed things at training and made it better and he put his own stamp on the club. But he was also big enough and smart enough to say he was new to the league and that when he felt he needed help or advice, he would ask for it. He's a very astute guy who knows how to get results and draw together all the different qualities of being a manager.

All this feelgood stuff came to an end for me at St Andrew's, ironically enough, when we played Coventry City there at the beginning of February (the Sky Blues were ground-sharing with Birmingham at the time). After about 15 minutes, I went up for a header with a defender and fell when I landed. I was in a crouch position and the defender landed on top of my Achilles. I felt my ankle fold out and back in. I'm sorry to state the obvious but it hurt like hell.

I try not to stay down as a point of principle. Don't show weakness. Don't show vulnerability. I got up and tried to run around a bit. Normally, after about 30 seconds, the pain goes away. This time, it didn't go away. I played the rest of the game anyway. We'd lost the previous game and I wanted to help us get some momentum back. I hit the bar with a header in the last minute, but the game ended goalless.

The manager was going to start me in the next match, a home game against Bristol City, but I didn't feel right and asked if I could be on the bench. We won the game 6–0 and I didn't get on, which was a relief because I was still in a lot of pain from the Achilles. I got it scanned the next day and they didn't like what they saw. They told me to put it in a medical boot straight away and wait for the opinion of a specialist.

It turned out I had 41 per cent damage to my Achilles. Don't ask me exactly what that means but apparently, if the tear gets to 45 per cent, it means instant surgery. I tore my calf too. The calf had tried to take over and compensate for what had happened to my heel. I'd made it a lot worse by insisting on staying on the field and trying to get a win over Coventry.

I had the meeting with the specialist a few days later. When I go into these medical rooms, I always go in there with the worst-case scenario in my head. I tell myself all my ligaments will be done, and I'll be out for six months, whatever. It's a protection mechanism, I suppose. And normally they say, 'It's not too bad, Troy, it's three weeks and you'll be fine, you could even play now if you want.'

This time, it wasn't like that. I knew there was a problem straight away because the doctor brought in another doctor, so there were two of them explaining what was going on. I don't know anything about medicine, but I do know that if it takes more than one person to explain what's going on, that's not a good sign.

As soon as the consultant, Andy Williams, saw my leg and my scan, he said, 'Sorry, mate, your season's over.' Tell a footballer that news with 20 games still to play and it feels like you have lost your whole season. As he went through the options about whether or not to have surgery I stayed calm, but as soon as I got in the car with my missus, I let it all out.

I was angry with myself. You start rethinking everything. I never had a pre-season because of all the stuff with West Brom and the stand-off with Watford. I was training on my own and that kind of stuff. Then I was training and playing ten days after everything had been resolved. I never gave myself a chance.

What if I'd had a pre-season? What if I had got fit properly? What if I hadn't been made to train with the Bomb Squad? What if I hadn't stayed on the pitch and turned what should have been six weeks out into five months? What if, what if, what if? I tortured myself with all those thoughts about what I could have done to avoid it happening. I know that's pointless, but I couldn't help it.

I chose not to have surgery. It's probably the longer route in terms of rebuild, but if you have surgery, there's no guarantee you'll come back to play. I had an injection to heal it and lifted weights to build the strength in the tendon. I chose that. My results have been so good the specialist wants to publish them because the results on the tendon are the best he has had so far.

But at the time, I felt really low. For the first time ever, I thought about quitting. I thought this could be the injury that makes me call it a day. Something else made it worse, too, and there's no point lying about this: I read a lot of the comments about me on social media and how people were reacting to the news that I was going to be out of the team for a prolonged period of time.

I wasn't getting much sympathy, put it that way. Watford went on a run soon after I was injured. We won ten of our next eleven games and so obviously people were saying I had been holding them back and now that I was out of action, the other lads had been liberated and we were able to play this fresh, vibrant style of football.

Well, hold on a second. Remember, we had a useless manager before and now we had a good manager. All the things that Xisco wanted were just starting to take shape when I got injured. I was out of the team at the very point where things were ready to accelerate.

The truth: you start reading all this garbage about 'Deeney's old and he's crap' and you start believing it. When you're in a lonely place, you start believing it. Then your weight starts going up and you can't control it and you're thinking, *What the hell's going on here?* You're eating well but you are getting heavier because you're not training.

I was lifting all the time. I had got to the point where I was lifting 240kg weights and that's what bodybuilders do. I was getting bigger and bigger until I was a big mountain and I couldn't seem to shake any of the weight. Sometimes I felt that I would never get back to the way I had been.

Watching was tough, even if we were doing well. The manager was great. He asked if I would travel to matches with the team and help him. He kept me involved. He would ask me advice about opposition players. He said he knew he could study data, but he wanted to know my opinions. So I felt like I got a little bit of a coaching role within the set-up and I was really grateful for that. I loved seeing some of our younger players blossoming.

Promotion, when it came, felt bitter-sweet. I had contributed but it didn't feel like it. It felt like I was the 18th man on the squad and I had just been watching the whole season. That was new to me, but I was so chuffed for everyone because being out of the Premier League had put a real financial strain on the football club and the staff who work for it. I could see the relief on the faces of the directors when we got promoted.

From a selfish point of view, I felt a little bit like everyone had forgotten about me. I'm just being honest about that. I think a lot of players feel like that when they're out injured. It can be difficult seeing a team prospering without you. You feel happy for the team and for the lads, but it is bound to make you feel a bit insecure. It's human nature.

But gradually, my spirits began to lift. When I got the all-clear that the tendon was good, I worked as hard as I could in pre-season. The thought of being back in the Premier League was great motivation for me. I lost two stone in the close season and for the people asking, 'Can he still do it, do we still need him, do we still want him?' I'll start scoring again and then you'll have your answer.

CHAPTER 17

FOOTBALL AND RACISM: NO MORE 'SHUT UP AND DRIBBLE'

I managed to get a couple of tickets for the Euro 2000 final between England and Italy in July 2021, and so Alisha and I drove down there and got to Wembley a couple of hours before kick-off. It meant a lot to me to be there. I had friends who were playing, and it felt like a massive moment for anybody who loves the England football team.

I noticed a change in the atmosphere long before we parked the car. All the excitement and the fun of this wonderful tournament (delayed a year by the Covid pandemic), all that post-lockdown sense of release and the 'Yay, it's coming home' stuff had curdled into something much more aggressive and threatening. The atmosphere outside the stadium was feral. Bottles were flying. People were being drenched in beer. There were flares and smoke. It smelled like trouble.

People came up to me, asking for autographs. And not in a way that meant I could refuse even if I'd wanted to. All the restraints had gone. People were drunk and off their heads on drugs. As I know, those things only accentuate the characteristics and the feelings a person has, so all their anger and all their insecurities came out.

One of the things I found interesting was how many people were using drugs openly, snorting cocaine off whatever surface they could find. All of them, as far as I could see, were either young or middle-aged white men but when I looked for the horror and the outrage about that in the newspapers and on television the next day, I couldn't find it.

Yes, there was widespread condemnation of the unruly scenes inside and outside the stadium and the way thugs without tickets had rushed disabled entrances and caused crushes and had occupied seats that did not belong to them once they had made their way inside the stadium. It was right that they should have been pilloried for the way they behaved.

But I didn't see anyone throwing up their arms in moral despair about the sight of people snorting cocaine in plain sight in close proximity to children. I'm sorry if this offends you, and I'm sorry if you think it's a marginal point, but I think the reason why the issue was not highlighted was because the people doing it were white.

If they had been young and middle-aged Black men snorting cocaine in public, it would have been presented as more evidence of the decay of Black society. It would have been presented as more evidence of broken Black Britain and its corrupting influence on the rest of the country. The condemnation would have been double or treble.

But because it was white men doing it, that didn't happen. There was even an undertone that taking cocaine is associated with affluence and therefore it is a status symbol. These were just lads having fun. They had bought the coke with their own hard-earned cash. There was a general feeling of people looking the other way about the drug-taking, both in the moment and in the media.

When the match ended, you knew you had seen the ugly head of English football rearing up again. It was as if the hooligans had wanted to remind us of something. 'We ain't left yet,' they were saying. 'Remember, guys, we're still here.' English football thought it had washed its hands of those people. It thought it had them on the run. The truth is, they never really went away.

The aftermath was predictable. I expected Jadon Sancho, Marcus Rashford and Bukayo Saka to be racially abused on social media after the penalty shoot-out. It was dispiriting, of course, but it was also inevitable because that is where we are in English society. For whatever reason, we have regressed. Racism was suppressed for a while, but it was only hiding underground. Now the racists are brave enough to come out into the daylight again.

The day after the game, I was frustrated that we were even talking about racism. I wasn't surprised, you weren't surprised, 90 per cent of the population weren't surprised about the racism issues. Can we start saying what we are going to do about it instead of falling over each other to condemn it? Because there is a danger that the noise people make when they say how terrible it is actually detracts from the issue. The noise camouflages the fact that nothing is being done.

The social media companies have to do more, yes, of course they do. But there is racism happening openly at football matches. In the stands and on the pitch. Our own governing bodies still don't have a set law in place to say that if you racially abuse a player like me, you will get a ten-game ban. It is down to an independent ruling – and we all know what the age bracket and the demographic of the magistrates and judges and administrators is.

Anti-racism is still fashionable right now but once it dies down a little bit, we won't have the power to keep asking what is the actual impact of what we are doing now. What are we doing to force change? It doesn't look like all the talking is doing much good.

It reinvigorated me in a way. It made me glad that everyone would realize how much work was still to be done. I had been having meetings with the Premier League and the FA to discuss the issue of whether players should continue taking the knee in the 2021–22 season. The gist of what I was asking them was: give me a reason why I should tell Watford players not to take the knee.

I mean, why would they want to stop now? What could I tell them has been achieved? Not an awful lot, as far as I can see. Some people point to that lack of action and say it is evidence that taking the knee is not working and therefore we should abandon it. Those are, generally speaking, people who oppose the whole concept of taking the knee and feel threatened by it.

The more logical response is that we keep taking the knee until something changes. And we go on and on. And I'm sorry if that makes the Premier League and the television companies uneasy and I'm sorry if it stops them pretending that everything's fine and everything's been fixed and that we've mended everything.

David McGoldrick, the Sheffield United and Republic of Ireland striker, was the one who suggested starting it in the English game at the beginning of Project Restart, when the Blades played the first game of the resumption at Aston Villa. But we'll keep doing it until change comes and when change comes, that's when we'll stop. That was why the players felt it necessary to release a statement at the beginning of August 2021 reiterating our commitment to taking the knee, even in the face of the booing that it attracted at times during the European Championships, when fans were back in the stadiums.

The statement had my wholehearted support. 'We feel now, more than ever,' it said, 'that it is important for us to continue to take the knee as a symbol of our unity against all forms of racism. We remain resolutely committed to our singular objective of eradicating racial prejudice wherever it exists, to bring about a global society of inclusion, respect and equal opportunities for all.'

Some people would undoubtedly have been more comfortable if we had stopped but they misunderstand the nature of protest. You don't stop protesting because you don't get anywhere to begin with. What sort of protest would that be? How shallow and weak would that make us seem? No, you keep on protesting until you make sure your voice is heard.

That is why it was important that Tyrone Mings criticized the Home Secretary, Priti Patel, who had poured scorn on footballers taking the knee some time earlier, when she condemned the racist abuse that had been aimed at Sancho, Saka and Rashford.

'You don't get to stoke the fire at the beginning of the tournament by labelling our anti-racism message as "Gesture Politics",' Tyrone wrote on Twitter, '& then pretend to be disgusted when the very thing we're campaigning against happens.'

I'm proud of players like Tyrone who speak out. The time's gone now when English footballers are going to keep quiet on race. The time's gone when we stay in our lane or listen to the type of person who once told LeBron James to 'shut up and dribble'. No thank you. We won't be doing that any more.

Colin Kaepernick, the American footballer who started taking the knee before NFL games while the national anthem was playing, was one of those who showed the way forward with that. The time has come when we must use the platform that we have to try to effect change and reform.

You see politicians who try to tell us, 'You should not mix football with politics' and yet those same politicians continue to speak on football matters. So it's okay for them to talk about it, but not us. They've done the same thing with Covid. They say, 'You guys all stay in your houses but we are going to go and do these G7 meetings and go to these places.'

The person who tells me to leave politics and race out of it will also tell me that I am a role model to their kids. If I am supposed to be a role model to your kids, I need to be conscious of all the things that would affect those kids. How am I supposed to know if I am a role model to a white kid, a Black kid, an Asian kid? I am a role model to all of them so I have to be who I am and show these kids that the curriculum in schools desperately needs to be updated.

And then there was the Matt Hancock situation when he was, shall we say, ignoring social-distancing rules. People tell us to behave and stay in when they are doing the opposite. There is a lot of pent-up frustration coming out from the players. We are at boiling point.

For a long time, throughout my childhood and my youth, I did not feel I was a victim of racial prejudice because I had white and Black families. I was given the talk: don't trust police; if you are ever stopped, use your manners; when you go into places, take your hood down because you will come under suspicion going into shops; stay away from the clothes rail, or they will think you are stealing something.

In our area, in Chelmsley Wood, it was a mix of Blacks, whites and Asians but we were all broke. I didn't see race as an issue until I moved further up the social chain. I went to buy my first car and walked into a fancy showroom in Watford in my tracksuit and hoodie. I couldn't get someone to come and talk to me until I took my hood down and they realized I was a footballer with money.

'Oh, Mr Deeney, do you want a cup of tea, please let us show you our top-of-the-range model.' I just turned around and left. He's got a hoodie on, he's Black, he probably hasn't got any money. Those are just the assumptions that are made about you when you are Black. At secondary school, I was aware of backhanded remarks.

When there was a group of Black kids, people called them a 'gang' of kids. When it was six white lads, they were a 'group' of kids.

As you get older, you see it more. I got my first proper car when I was at Watford. It was an all-white C-class Mercedes and in my eyes, it was the business. I was out driving with my mate, a Spanish kid, in the car, and we pulled up at a shop. A police car drove past and my mate noticed they were staring at us. They came back, stopped and asked if it was my car.

They asked what I did and scoffed when I said I was a footballer. They asked my name and I told them they already knew my name because they had already run the search on me. You get to know the routine. You are driving a car and you know you are going to get pulled over, you walk into a shop and you know security are watching. Issues of race have always been there.

When George Floyd was murdered on 25 May 2020, it sparked something in me. It was during the pandemic and we were all at home, we all saw the news, we all saw this video lasting 9 minutes 29 seconds of a man being murdered. There is no way that anyone could deny that. It was racial murder. Like a lot of other people, I think, it made me angry. It made me decide I had to speak up more.

When George Floyd was murdered, I saw all the activity on social media and big companies posting black squares to show solidarity – or to protect their brand – and I thought, *Is that all we are going to do? Is that it? Are we just going to post on social media and then go back into the bubble? We need to have a bit more value about ourselves than to leave it at that, surely.*

It's something I feel passionately about. Martin Luther King and Malcolm X, that was the 1960s, but we talk about it like it was in Egyptian times. In the early 2020s, we are still very close to what racial segregation looked like. There are people in their seventies who lived through that. I'd hate to think that 60 years from now, my kids might still be having the same conversation about the need for progress.

If I tell them when they grow up that they need to be active and I had done nothing about it, then I would be a hypocrite.

Do I think people are outwardly racist in this country? Certainly not everybody. But do I think people don't understand when they are being racist? Yes, of course I do. My consciousness of race issues has grown. I am interested in people and stories. I have read books on Putin, books on Hitler, what made him think like that. I try not just to read books that will confirm my own view.

Not long after George Floyd was murdered and the world was in uproar about it, the 20 captains of the Premier League clubs and five or six officials from the Premier League itself had a final Zoom meeting about Project Restart. There were six items on the agenda and the sixth of those was 'race and our stance on it moving forwards'. I texted Wes Morgan, the Leicester captain, and said it would be interesting to see how the league approached that.

In the weeks that preceded that Zoom call, we had acted swiftly and decisively about other pressing issues. Everyone was united about the desire to pay tribute, both financially and symbolically, to the NHS and we decided to sell shirts off, donate part of our wages and have badges on our shirts and messaging at our stadiums.

There was never a discussion about that kind of stuff. Everyone was in agreement. It was the same when we had rainbow laces. There was no discussion. This is what we're doing. There was no dissension. None was expected and none was forthcoming. I don't remember us even having a call about it. The Premier League stands with it. This is what we're doing. It was, quite rightly, a *fait accompli*.

Then about a week before we went back, there was this one last Zoom call. Everyone was training. Wes and I texted as the meeting was happening. The final point on the agenda was about racism, but as we got to it, it felt like the meeting was being wrapped up. I don't think it was a deliberate attempt to avoid the conversation. I genuinely think it's such an uncomfortable topic for some people that they do their best to avoid it and sometimes that's subconscious.

I texted Wes. 'Are these guys serious?' I told him I was going to put my hand up and I told him he had to back me up. So I unmuted myself and went off on my rant. I said we had a big platform and a huge opportunity. The world had been rocked by protests in the wake of the George Floyd murder. Later that summer, NBA players would refuse to play a play-off match but even now sports stars were making protests. I thought this was a time, especially when racial abuse of our own footballers was on the rise, when we needed to make a stand.

My stance was that we needed to do something as a collective, as a league, because otherwise what we were going to get was individual teams making their own protests and it would reflect badly on the Premier League. I knew there would be support for protest at Watford, but this was about the whole. It would be much more powerful if we could get the whole Premier League on board with all the bigger clubs involved.

I said I felt ashamed we weren't even talking about it. Some of the officials got a bit jumpy then and said they had been about to talk about it, but I reminded them they had got to the end of the conversation. I said I understood it was difficult to address. I said we needed to do something. We had all come together for the NHS. I said it would be nice if there were a consensus. I thought we were dodging it.

I spoke for about eight minutes and then I took a deep breath and I muted myself and there was an awkward few seconds where I thought, *Fuck, I wonder how that's going to go down?* Then Seamus Coleman jumped in and said he thought it was something we needed to do and that Everton would support it.

Then Kevin De Bruyne came in and said, 'I'm with Troy.' He said the Manchester City players had been thinking about it and talking about it with Raheem Sterling. He said they had discussed changing the names on the back of the shirt for a slogan. Jordan Henderson said, 'I'm with Troy.' Everyone joined in. I went from nervousness to being proud. All these guys had been thinking it, but I had articulated it.

Jordan Henderson is the most organized man I have ever met in my life and at that point, he suggested we should have a separate captains' call, come up with some ideas and present back to the Premier League. On that call, Kevin suggested removing individual names from the back of the shirt and substituting them with the slogan Black Lives Matter.

I said we should change the Premier League badge on the sleeve to Black Lives Matter as well, shoot for the stars, and put a package together. Mark Noble sorted out some stuff with eBay about auctioning off the shirts and eBay were great about not taking fees. Some of it was left to me and Wes and I drove it forward with my missus, who is a graphic designer.

She did all the designs for the badge and drew them up within a few hours. We substituted the A in 'Black' for a clenched fist of solidarity. It's funny when you talk about race: you want something that's really bold and really powerful and makes a statement but doesn't offend anybody. It is a really difficult balance to strike.

And the great thing about us all acting together was, if Troy Deeney and Wes Morgan spoke about it, it wasn't going to happen. But when I got Kevin De Bruyne, Harry Kane, Jordan Henderson going, 'We're with Troy', it made change. It needs everybody to pull together just like we did later with the European Super League. Look at how all the fans came together to oppose the plans for the ESL and it fell down like a house of cards.

The badge was a difficult sell to the Premier League because they have never allowed that before. The final meeting was a couple of days before the resumption of the season, with the Aston Villa–Sheffield United game. I texted Wes and said we had to go strong. The players had come to the decision we had to put 'Black Lives Matter' on the back of the shirts and that there could be no compromise. On that final call, I felt the Premier League were nervous it would set a precedent and open the floodgates for more protest badges.

They were worried about not mixing football with politics, but my argument was that when Matt Hancock turned around and asked footballers to do more for the NHS, is that not mixing football with politics? A politician had crossed that line and called us out for not doing enough. He had crossed the line so there is no line now. So we played the first round of 12 games with 'Black Lives Matter' on our backs and on a badge.

We played for the rest of that season with 'Black Lives Matter' on our shirt sleeves and in September 2020, the Premier League announced that it would be replaced with a badge that said 'No Room for Racism' and that the Premier League badge itself would be reinstated. It's a lot safer for them. I understand that.

I don't know if they would have agreed to it now. Probably not. The Black Lives Matter slogan itself has become more controversial since reactionaries, right-wingers and racists worked themselves up into a frenzy of outrage that footballers were actually demonstrating their support for the Black Lives Matter political movement in the US that supports defunding the police and aligns itself with Marxist–Leninism.

That idea is so funny, so hilarious, that I laugh about it every time I see some Tory politician or some GB News presenter spouting it. I love the idea that footballers, who are just about the most conservative group of people you could ever meet and who think they already pay enough tax, would support a Marxist-Leninist movement. They would run an absolute mile from that.

What frustrates me about it more than anything is that it is being deliberately misunderstood. We are not supporting the organization, but we are absolutely supporting the idea that *Black lives matter*. And quite frankly, if you object to the idea that Black lives matter then I would like to hear from you in person. Actually, come to think of it, I probably have heard from you in person when you've been racially abusing me on Twitter.

People are spreading misinformation. How many times have we spoken out and said, 'It's not that, it's not that, it's not that'? The answer is over and over and over again. There have been press releases to say that we are not supporting the organization, from Harry Kane, to Tyrone Mings to myself. You see the hypocrisy throughout all that.

The same people who were booing Raheem Sterling and saying he was awful a couple of years ago are now saying he's great when he scores. They are the same people who said that if Sterling scored, it was 0–0, because anything he did didn't count. They pick and choose when it's acceptable to talk about race. They pick and choose when it's acceptable to even like Black players.

You look in the media – and I know I work in the media – but when people are talking about how good Kalvin Phillips is, why are there stories in the paper about how his Jamaican dad is in jail? They say they are just giving you a backstory but that backstory could have been given a few years ago when he burst on to the scene. It's very particular and spiteful in the way it is done.

You can't understand the connotations of that unless you have suffered it yourself. How am I supposed to know how a gay couple feels? How a bisexual man feels or how a transgender woman feels? I don't know. Until you have been in those shoes, it is very difficult.

I find it hugely amusing when people say there is no racism in this country. We are so ignorant as English people. The racism is still here. There was that trial in Birmingham in April 2021 over the killing of the former footballer Dalian Atkinson by the police. It barely got mentioned in the media. It is not comfortable to talk about it. It was not fashionable. It was barely newsworthy. I heard more about Cristiano Ronaldo removing two Cokes from the front of his press conference during the Euros than the killing of Dalian Atkinson.

Then there was that tragedy with the murder of a young woman, Sarah Everard, who was killed by the Metropolitan Police officer. There was a public outcry, demonstrations, vigils, manhunts. It was good to see everyone coming together for justice – that's the way it should be. But would her killing have generated the same headlines, would there have been a vigil, if she were Black?

You have to keep developing the conversation. The Civil Rights movement started in the 1960s. We are now 60 years on. We can't expect there to be monumental change to a point where we are all treated equally in the space of months since the taking the knee movement started. More conversations are taking place although, a lot of the time, we are still having the same conversation.

You know the other thing I love? White people trying to tell Black people how they should protest about racism. 'You can do it but just don't do it that way. You can protest but don't have Black Lives Matter on your shirt. That's wrong. Do it another way. Use a different slogan. Then it'll be all right with us.' So what should we do? Should we riot?

I do think that part of the problem is that the discourse has become polarized. You are either vegan and woke or you are racist. You can't be in the middle. It's black and white, there can't be any grey area. That's where the world has got to.

I want to get away from wokeism versus extremism. I want us to get some sanity back in our society. I don't want to be a vegan but that doesn't mean I hate vegans. It's okay to say, 'I respect you for your decision but I like meat.'

Unfortunately, the coronavirus crisis has only exaggerated the polarization of the discussion. It has amplified everyone's frustrations and negative energies and it is all coming out in anything they disagree with. People say they are sick of being told what is right and what is wrong and they are making their own decision.

It all makes me think we are getting very close to a critical stage in the fight against racial abuse in football. In the 2021–22 Premier League season, fans are back and even though football has been like a shadow sport without them, some supporters have been yearning to get back so they can hurl abuse again. When things go bad, they are going to say what they really think because everyone has been trapped and caged in for so long.

Say Arsenal are playing out from the back: in 2020–21, it was acceptable because everyone was watching from home and they could only tweet and type. Say Rob Holding makes a mistake: do you think everyone's going to say, 'Oh well, at least he's trying.' No, they're not. Football is their release.

And when players take the knee before a game, what will happen? We already had a sneak preview of that here and there at the back end of last season and during the Euros in the summer of 2021. Are you prepared for that to start again? Because believe me, it is an issue that can't be simply wished away.

We need to see the Premier League and the football authorities and the government stepping up because we need real change, not just badges and fine words. The week before the start of the 2021–22 season, the Premier League announced they would be introducing 'enhanced anti-discrimination measures' including bans for racially abusive behaviour. Again, it sounded good in theory but it offered very little detail.

There were no promises of changes in legislation. There was nothing of real note. If a fan racially abuses a player and it is reported, is there a standard punishment that is in place or is it all on individual clubs and players to change a club's mind and then the Premier League will take all the credit for it? The Premier League statement didn't answer those questions. I think we are getting very close to that stage where we are going to see a lot of frustration come out.

Let's say Raheem misses a sitter, say when Man City play Spurs, do you not think he's going to get reminded how crap he is and how Black he is? What has changed on the face of it that you can see? I would like very simple, clear things. The bans for players racially abusing opponents have to get bigger. A lot bigger. Eight games doesn't scare anyone. I would make it so any player found guilty of racial abuse has to pay the fine himself, not the club.

The player has to go on an educational course, and it has to be real. What happens on the course, who is delivering it, who is he talking to? If a fan is found guilty of racially abusing a player, online or otherwise, there should be a minimum two-year ban.

If you take your kids to a game and then you have to stop taking your kids because you have racially abused someone, your kids are going to start asking you questions and it's going to get embarrassing. We have to do things that shame people, not to the point that they are publicly persecuted, but we have to have rules and regulations that are in place that frighten people.

If I make a bad tackle, I know the parameters for the punishment for me. But if you abuse me, nobody knows. It's a grey area. Make it a minimum ten games. That might stop people. It might at least make them think. Sometimes the person who reports the abuse pays a heavier price in the long term than the abuser. They are the ones left with a reputation – he's awkward, he's difficult – not the abuser.

In September 2020, remember, Leeds made their goalkeeper, Kiko Casilla, club captain for a game a few months after he received an eight-match Football Association ban and a £60,000 fine for racially abusing the forward Jonathan Leko in a game against Charlton a year earlier.

He could pay that fine. It's lumpy but he could pay it. It won't affect him in the grand scheme of things. That also tells me that the club doesn't take it seriously. You've got young Black players coming through and they are going to turn around and question the justice of that.

Things like that are part of the reason why it's important we keep taking the knee and keep doing it until there is real change, until we shame people into taking real action. My only hesitation – although perhaps it's better to call it a frustration – is when I compare what we are trying to do with the uproar over the European Super League earlier this year.

When a few clubs started to worry their money was going to disappear and that they were going to be left behind by the Big Six, everyone acted immediately, on the click of their fingers. It was 'fix it, fix it, fix it'. But when you ask to make simple changes for racism, the response is that it is a long process, it is legislation, it is complicated.

If you can do it to protect your money, why can't you do it to protect a swathe of your players? I would prefer the authorities to say, 'No, we're not interested in change.' At least then we're honest. And we know how the land lies. But instead they say, 'No, we really want change, we're really passionate about this, we want to be with you guys.' But every time you put ideas together, there is push back.

I am on various boards with Ian Wright and we have to calm

each other down. It is not because we are hostile, it's because we are frustrated with the lack of movement. We speak about the same stuff every month and nothing seems to move forward. By observing the gesture, sometimes that becomes an excuse for these organizations to do nothing meaningful.

If we get radical, like people did with the European Super League, and we say, 'Forget it, we're not playing,' that will make people change. If we start walking off the pitch when a teammate is racially abused, that will make people change. The Premier League will go, 'Oh shit, we need to do something now.' But why do we need to get to that point? Why do we need to get to a crisis point? Let's deal with it beforehand.

There are some signs of progress, there are some signs of ambivalence, there are some signs of regression and there are some signs of bigotry. Part of the problem is that the discussion has become so polarized and so aggressive and so intolerant. We need to get back to a point where we can discuss things rationally again. It seems like a land far away.

AFTERWORD:
LIFE ISN'T A PRISON ANY MORE

Redemption? There is a finality to that that implies I have done everything I wanted to do, that I have recovered, that I will never err again and now I am redeemed. Now I can sit back, and everything is finished. Well, it is not quite like that.

What it means, for me, is that I am closing the chapter on all the old stuff, the bad things, the hurt, the pain, the strife. And prison. I am not going back to jail. Life isn't a prison any more for me and I hope I don't have to talk about it in that way again.

Whether I'm redeemed, ultimately, has to be judged by others. Redemption, for me, is about both being forgiven for all the bad things I've done and being able to forgive other people for the bad things they've done to me. I'm happy with my side of that bargain. I've forgiven everybody except Sperm Donor. He's the only one who will never be forgiven.

He doesn't hurt me any more. He used to hurt me but he can't hurt me any more. I can't forgive him, mainly for my Mum. I see everything she went through when I was a kid and I think that, even if you're not around, the minimum you should do as a parent, the absolute minimum you should do, is contribute financially to your child's welfare.

There are no excuses for doing what he did unless there is a complete breakdown between the parents. When you have got a willing parent, like my Mum, who's saying you can see the kid whenever you want, there's no excuse. When I saw my Mum having to work two or three jobs, there's no coming back from that. Not as far as I'm concerned.

My Mum is more accepting. She is more forgiving of people, even if they have hurt her. She knows him and she knows how his life has gone. She has realized that's just who he is. He's not a stick-around dad. He's a floater, he's a go-wherever-the-wind-takes-him kind of guy.

My Mum's older. She's got her own foundations. She always had her Dad there. I had a Dad there but I always felt I was missing something. We may have everything but we still fixate on what we don't have. I think that's a sentiment a lot of people can appreciate.

Yeah, Sperm Donor damaged me, but I think the damage is beautiful, to be honest. The damage has created who I am. My inner strength and determination have come from that. There is fragility within that, of course. There are moments I am weak because of that. The bigger thing is that I just don't respect him and if I don't respect him, I can't like him.

There are people I can't stand with a passion, but I respect them. Whether that be for their line of work, where they have got to in life or the way they look after their kids. You have to have something to cling on to have a little bit of respect for that person. I have absolutely zero respect for Sperm Donor.

My Mum has been the biggest influence on me as a person, though. Because of the unconditional love she showed me. No matter what, despite all the bad stuff we went through and the low times, I never once felt like we weren't going to be okay. My Dad was the one who made me a sportsman. He took me out with a football, bought me a Pelé video. Life in general has shaped and hardened who I am and given me the mental toughness that helped me succeed as a footballer.

My Dad and I are actually similar parents in some ways. For all his faults, I knew my Dad loved me, just like I love my kids, Myles, 12, Isla, 7, Amelia, 6, and Clay, who is 18 months old. The main difference is I am financially able to look after my kids and keep them safe.

I parent similar to my Dad in terms of manners, respect and what I'll stand for and won't stand for. He was able to give more time for me. He was able to go out all weekend and play football and do whatever we needed to do. I am not able to do that. My parenting skills are more about the finances than the time I can give. I can't give time. We train six days a week, seven days a week sometimes.

Do I regret that? There are times when I wish I could be with them more, of course, but the regret gets outweighed when I sit back and look at the life I have provided for them and the opportunities they have. It might not make up for the lost time, but it gives them a platform to go on and be better in their lives. I hope it shows them that you have to work hard, you have to make sacrifices to get what you want.

I don't think I'll struggle when my football career ends. I'll quit when I've lost the love for it. I won't quit when I'm dropping down the leagues. It's when the passion's gone for it or the body has given up on me. That's when I'll quit. The game's getting younger. Once you start realizing that people are running all over you, you go, 'That's not for me.'

I have so many interests outside of football that I think I should be all right. I can just be Dad and push my kids as hard as they want to go. If they want to be sports people or academics, I'll push them and turn into that awkward Dad who is always urging them on by the side of the pitch.

I am the happiest I've been in my adult life. When you are a kid, you don't know anything about social responsibilities or bills, it's all about you. You can be selfish. But as an adult, this is as good as it gets. My partner is unbelievably good for me. She enhances who I am. She pushes me to be better at the good things I do rather than highlighting the things I do wrong. The kids are happy, the missus is fantastic, and I am getting into that space now where everybody around me is starting to understand where I am and I am starting to have conversations that allow people in.

I know it would be easy to go back to the way I was before, to court trouble, to flirt with disaster. I fight that fight every day, to avoid slipping back into the old habits. I fight not to revert to those old traits. It is a dangerous slope, that, because it takes only one night to fall. It takes the rest of your life to be strong.